PAUL'S PASTORAL VISION

PAUL'S
PASTORAL
VISION

**Pastoral Letters for a
Pastoral Church Today**

REV. WILLIAM F. MAESTRI

ALBA · HOUSE   NEW · YORK

SOCIETY OF ST. PAUL, 2187 VICTORY BLVD., STATEN ISLAND, NEW YORK 10314

Library of Congress Cataloging-in-Publication Data

Maestri, William.
    Paul's pastoral vision: pastoral letters for a pastoral church
today / by William F. Maestri.
       p.   cm.
    Bibliography: p.
    ISBN 0-8189-0556-5
    1. Bible, N.T. Pastoral Epistles — Criticism, interpretation.
etc. 2. Pastoral theology — Biblical teaching. 3. Paul the
Apostle, Saint. I. Title.
BS2735.6.P45M34   1989
227'.8306 — dc19   89-203
                                          CIP

Nihil Obstat:
Rev. Reginald R. Masterson, O.P.
Censor Librorum

Imprimatur:
† Most Rev. Philip M. Hannan
Archbishop of New Orleans
December 1, 1988

Designed, printed and bound in the United States of
America by the Fathers and Brothers of the
Society of St. Paul, 2187 Victory Boulevard,
Staten Island, New York 10314, as part of their
communications apostolate.

Printing Information:

Current Printing - first digit   1   2   3   4   5   6   7   8   9   10   11   12

Year of Current Printing - first year shown
1989   1990   1991   1992   1993   1994   1995   1996

Dedication

For Thomas Perrier, OSB
a true friend

TABLE OF CONTENTS

INTRODUCTION

The Catholic existential philosopher, Gabriel Marcel, makes a distinction between a problem to be solved and a mystery which invites self-surrender. This is a distinction with a difference. Too often, we fail to make this crucial distinction and attempt to turn "the great mysteries" into problems. The result is violence.

We moderns pride ourselves on problem-solving, from placing a man on the moon to the miracles of modern medicine; the method of science; the power of technology; human intelligence and creativity; and money. To view life as simply a problem to be solved means that we subtract from life its grace and wonder. In time, we shall come to know not only good and evil, but *all* things will be under our control. There will be no more gaps to fill. God will become a useless illusion. We will come of age and God will be dismissed. All things appear possible. A new age and a new humanity will appear.

Yet this drive for problem-solving and extending our control has not produced the expected happiness. In fact, humankind has become diseased with its success. Too often, the work of our hands has produced new and more troubling questions. For example, we know that the atoms for peace now speak of the total war; the increased industrialization of our society has also increased pollution; and the miracles of medicine also raise profound moral issues concerning the dignity and destiny of the human person.

In his first encyclical, *Redemptor Hominis (The Redeemer of Man*, 1979), Pope John Paul II wrote:

'If, then, our age, that is, the period of the present
generation as the end of the second millennium draws
near, seems a time of splendid progress, it shows itself
simultaneously to be full of imminent dangers to the
human race. The Church must speak of these dangers to
all persons of good will and be zealous in discussing
them. For the present state of the human race seems out
of harmony with what the moral order objectively requires, namely justice, and especially social love for our
fellow human beings.

These words offer a profound reminder that technological
progress must never be purchased at the price of the dignity of
the human person. If such is allowed, then our progress is, in
reality, a threat.

While not denying the tremendous and stunning advance
of science and technology, we must also appreciate "the other
dimension" which cannot be classified or quantified. That is,
we humans live with mystery. And, as St. Augustine reminds
us, we are a mystery to ourselves. Large and significant dimensions of life speak to us (at times even shout) about the gratuity
and contingency of human existence. The sheer fact of our
personal existence is a gift. The sheer fact that one day we shall
be no more reminds us of our finitude. Mystery reminds us that
we are not in total control of our lives. Significant moments and
episodes escape our methods and techniques. We can only
stand in awe and wonder. Only in such a stance of openness
can we move from knowledge to wisdom, from intelligence to
love.

The awareness of the mystery and wonder of existence
moves us to a thirst for a deeper appreciation of our dignity and
destiny. Through the work of the Holy Spirit and grace, we are
moved to seek Jesus Christ and the Church. We find ourselves
asking the question of the first disciples in the fourth Gospel:
"Where do you live?" Jesus' answer is for us as well: "Come
and see" (Jn 1:39). It is only in following and seeing Jesus that
we come to lovingly and truthfully see who we are. Jesus Christ
is *the* answer to the mystery and the problem of being human.

Jesuit theologian Rene Latourelle, S.J. has written with deep insight about the meaning of Jesus for the meaning of human existence. In his profound work, *Man and His Problems in the Light of Jesus Christ*, Father Latourelle has written:

> I too am convinced that Christ, and Christ alone, gives *meaning* not only to the human condition as a whole, by explaining to human beings their vocation as children called by grace to the life and glory of God, but also to the human condition in its main details, by shedding light on the concrete, particular problems affecting it. He alone is the piercing Light that illumines man through and through and reveals him to himself. In Christ, who is pure Light, man discovers the ultimate truth of his own being.

The Jesus who reveals the meaning and truth of our human existence is himself truly human. God in Christ does not remain external to our history and condition but out of love becomes our poor flesh (Jn 1:14). It is the Church which continues in time, and points to that time beyond time, the "dangerous memory" of Jesus. This "dangerous memory" is proclaimed, celebrated, and offered to the world in hope: "For God so loved the world that he gave his only Son, that whoever believes in him should not perish but have eternal life" (Jn 3:16).

To speak of the human person and Jesus as the one who reveals what it means to be truly human also involves us in speaking about the Church, not as a problem to be solved, but as a mystery which continues to reveal the unbounded love of God. Like Jesus, the Church is both human and divine — divine in its origin and destiny; human in its earthly, historical pilgrimage. The sinless, stainless Bride is a hope and a promise. The all too human sinfulness of its members serves as a constant reminder of Christ. This paradox and mystery of the People of God is beautifully expressed by the Apostle Paul writing to the Christians at Corinth:

> But we have this treasure in earthen vessels, to show that the transcendent power belongs to God and not to us. We are afflicted in every way, but not crushed; perplexed,

but not driven to despair; persecuted, but not forsaken;
struck down, but not destroyed; always carrying in the
body the death of Jesus, so that the life of Jesus may also
be manifest in our bodies. For while we live we are always
being given up to death for Jesus' sake, so that the life of
Jesus may be manifested in our mortal flesh. (2 Cor
4:7-11)

Pope Paul VI, in his opening statement at the second
session of the Second Vatican Council, said: "The Church is a
mystery. It is a reality imbued with the hidden presence of
God. It lies, therefore, within the very nature of the Church to
be always open to new and greater exploration." The *Dogmatic
Constitution on the Church (Lumen Gentium)* opens with the
recognition that the Church is a mystery, that is, a divine
reality which cannot be totally explained in human terms. The
identity of the Church is a mystery of the Church. In the words
of *Lumen Gentium,*

By her relationships with Christ, the Church is a kind of
sacrament or sign of intimate union with God, and of the
unity of all mankind . . . The mystery of the holy Church
is manifest in her very foundation, for the Lord Jesus
inaugurated her by preaching the good news, that is, the
coming of God's Kingdom, which, for centuries, had
been promised in the Scriptures: "The time is fulfilled,
and the kingdom of God is at hand." (Mk 1:15; cf. Mt
4:17)

Part of the mystery of the Church is its human reality. The
Church celebrates the Eucharist with a hope toward the
"Christ who will come again." There is a provisionality, an
incompleteness, and a tension about the Church. The Second
Vatican Council was not unmindful of the pilgrim nature of the
Church. "The Church, to which we are called in Christ Jesus,
and in which we acquire sanctity through the grace of God, will
attain her full perfection only in the glory of heaven." The
Church as mystery is "both/and." The Church is both institu-

tional and mystical; sinful and full of grace; historical and always pointing to an Absolute Future who is God. The mystery and paradox of the Church is expressed by the Lutheran pastor and theologian, Richard John Neuhaus:

> The Council's renewed understanding of the Church in historical terms was protected from a loss of transcendence because of its recovered focus on the *telos* of history, the Church in the glory of the Kingdom. The Church is everything that it appears to be in history, and much more. It is both the Church militant (*ecclesia militans*) here in time and the Church triumphant (*ecclesia triumphans*) in glory. As Augustine viewed the Church on earth as the lesser and inferior part of the Church, so we too can see the Church as a pilgrim community to what it truly is. We say "truly is" and not simply "truly will be," for all things most truly are their "end in the process of becoming." Only in this light may believers say such extravagant (preposterous?) things about the Church. Said now, such statements are paradoxical, but it is paradox that will be superseded and vindicated in the fulfillment of the promise of the conclusion of the pilgrimage. (*The Catholic Moment*)

The divine and historical aspects of the Church must be accepted and loved. Such an acceptance and love for the Church requires us to be what Father Karl Rahner, S.J. calls the "ecclesial Christian." We must resist premature closure as to the identity, mission, and destiny of the Church. We must resist the idolatry of those who would totally identify the Church with the Kingdom of God. Likewise, we must resist the idolatry of those who would identify the Church with some earthly power or political agenda. In both idolatries, the Church of transcendent hope is eliminated and a different Gospel is proclaimed. Father Rahner writes the following about being an ecclesial Christian:

> An ecclesial Christian of this kind must of course be aware of the historicity of the Church. He knows therefore about all the far-too-human and inhuman aspects of what

has happened in the Church . . . A Christian who believes
that the Church truly comes from Jesus Christ and consequently that it is the basic sacrament of salvation for the
whole world, in the face of this only too often very human
history of the Church, cannot simply ingenuously point to
other historical structures and appeal to the fact that it is
a history of feeble human beings . . . what he ought to do
is to hope and expect the victory of grace, which the
Church even in its visible manifestation is meant to
promise to the world, to be revealed in radiant splendor in
its own history. ("Courage for an Ecclesial Christianity")

The Second Vatican Council not only spoke of the Church
as a mystery but also of a Church with a pastoral mission
(*Pastoral Constitution on the Church in the Modern World,
Gaudium et Spes*). That is, the Church is entrusted with the
good news of Jesus Christ and proclaims that good news to all
men and women of good will. The Gospel proclamation is such
that it also recognizes what is good in culture and society. The
Church, proclaiming the Gospel and encouraging what is
humanly good, seeks to lead all to Christ. As a pilgrim people
travelling through history on the way to the new Jerusalem, the
Church preaches, teaches, and gives public witness to our
hope — Jesus as Crucified and Risen. In the words of
Gaudium et Spes:

> . . . This Second Vatican Council, having probed more
> profoundly into the mystery of the Church, now addresses
> itself without hesitation, not only to the sons of the
> Church and to all who invoke the name of Christ, but to
> the whole of humanity. For the Council yearns to explain
> to everyone how it conceives of the presence and activity
> of the Church in the world today.

The Church, with this pastoral mission, is one which
desires to hear the questions that anguish humankind and
desires to offer the loving acceptance of God in Christ.

The importance of the documents on the Church cannot
be over-estimated. The Church is a mystery and a community

with a mission to the world in the name of God's salvific will. Yet another document claims our attention, namely, the *Dogmatic Constitution on Divine Revelation (Dei Verbum)*. So much of the Church's identity, mission, and hope is contained in the revealed word of God. The gracious God who revealed himself in Jesus also revealed himself in Holy Scripture and, through the Holy Spirit, continues to reveal himself to each new generation in and through the Church. The word of God is not simply a collection of interesting books, historical accounts, or beautiful poetry. The word of God is active and alive in the life of the Church and the Christian. To be ignorant of the Scriptures is to be ignorant of the person of Jesus and the mission of the Church. *Dei Verbum* speaks with power and eloquence concerning the place of Sacred Scripture in the life of the Church. "The Church has always venerated the divine Scriptures just as she venerates the body of the Lord, since from the table of both the word of God and the body of Christ she unceasingly receives and offers to the faithful the bread of life, especially in the sacred liturgy."

The Church as both mystery and grace is nourished in its pastoral mission by Scripture. The Council, in *Dei Verbum*, continually encourages a reading, praying, and studying of God's word. This is especially necessary for the priest who is entrusted with the ministry of preaching and teaching. In the words of the Apostle Paul: "But how are men to call upon him in whom they have not believed? And how are they to believe in him of whom they have not heard? And how are they to hear without a preacher? And how can men preach unless they are sent?" (Rm 10:14-15).

The pastoral mission of the Church is not simply one of telling others about Christ and the power of his resurrection. The pastoral mission of the Church, like charity, must include, in a primary way, the community of faith. The Church is never above or exempt from the judging and healing Gospel she preaches. The Church is that "little flock" which remains in the world calling the world to realize its destiny within the loving plan of God. This calling of the world to its true destiny

becomes believable to the extent that Jesus is proclaimed as
Lord in spirit and truth within the Church. Hence, the Church
itself has pastoral needs as well as a pastoral mission. Part of
the mystery of this pastoral Church is the recognition that *it* is
sinful, incomplete, and provisional. Yet, at the same time, this
pastoral Church is also the Church entrusted with the Gospel.

Throughout this book, we will examine some of the anxie-
ties, hurts, and confusions of the Church. Our examination
will always be done in the spirit of seeking the truth with love.
In looking at the concerns of the Church, we are also looking at
ourselves. The looking is not done from the stance of an
objective, disinterested observer, but from one who is committed to *this* Church. To examine our concerns within the
Church is not to engage in a morbid self-destruction, but to
grow ever more into the full stature of Christ. Our problems are
also our opportunities because "in all these things we are more
than conquerors through him who loved us" (Rm 8:37).

The present concerns of the Church are many but not
unfamiliar. The people of God live within a living tradition and
stand on the shoulders of our ancestors in faith. We are part of
a great crowd of witnesses from whom we have much to learn.
In our discussion, we shall turn to a great Christian pastor —
Paul. We shall hold up "a distant mirror" so as to better
understand our present and move with hope into the future.
The pastoral needs of our Church will be viewed through the
letters of Paul (I and II Timothy and Titus). We will, hopefully,
not engage in a mindless repetition of the past nor engage in a
mindless rejection of the past simply because it is our past.
Rather, we want to engage in a "march of wisdom" by which we
come to possess the living faith of the dead and not the dead
faith of the living. Simply put, there is much in the pastoral
letters of Paul which speaks to our present situation.

What follows unfolds in a rather simple manner. The first
chapter provides a brief overview of the pastoral letters. We
shall then turn our attention to some of the major themes in the
pastoral letters as they relate to our pastoral concerns today. To
be specific, we shall examine the need for leadership for a

pastoral Church. Special emphasis will be placed on the style and character of the community leader. Next, we shall explore the role of tradition and teaching within the Church. We want to develop a teaching which respects the living tradition of the Church while at the same time applying that tradition to the concerns of today. This teaching task is crucial, for in an age of the mass media, the Gospel is continually being challenged by "earthly Gospels."

Faithful teaching bespeaks a teacher who is faithful. Special consideration must be given to the one who teaches in the name of the faith community. Religious instruction (catechesis) has become a major concern in the Church today. In chapter three, we will offer some reflections on the teaching ministry in the Church. This ministry of teaching extends from the hierarchy, to the theological community, through the parish, school, and family levels.

Chapter four is concerned with the moral life. Believable teaching requires a public witness. We must live daily what we profess. We must give evidence that Jesus is not an ideal we know about, but a living person in our individual and community lives. Before we ask what we are to do, we must ask what kind of person we are to be. The moral life is more (but never less) than rules and regulations. The moral life is being transformed in the life of Christ. Such a transformation takes place within a community over the whole of one's life. The local parish, the family, and the school are these communities of virtue and vision which tell and retell the stories of Jesus.

Chapter five raises the important question of vocation — vocation and ministry. The Second Vatican Council called the laity to assume an active role in the life of the Church. The *Decree on the Apostolate of the Laity (Apostolicam Actuositatem)* spoke eloquently of the lay vocation:

> For by its very nature the Christian vocation is also a vocation to the apostolate. No part of the structure of a living body is merely passive but each has a share in the function as well as in the life of the body. So, too, in the body of Christ, which is the Church, the whole body,

"according to the functioning in due measure of each
single part, derives its increase" (Ep 4:16). . . The
member who fails to make his proper contributions to the
development of the Church must be said to be useful
neither to the Church nor to himself.

Honesty requires that we acknowledge the presence of a
vocation and identity crisis, not only with the laity, but with the
clergy. Unfortunately, the increased activity and responsibility of the laity have been seen by some as a threat to the identity
and work of the priest. This notion of a "diminished priesthood" has caused much pain and confusion for those within the
clergy and for those whom they serve. Yet the priest continues
to be seen by the laity as essential to the life of the Church and
their spiritual growth in Christ. Father Andrew Greeley, who
has conducted extensive research on the Catholic Church in
America, offers the following:

> . . . the most striking finding of both the 1974 study of the
> adult Catholic population and the 1979 study of young
> Catholics is that priests are still of enormous importance
> to Catholics. Indeed the strongest correlation of Church
> attendance and Catholic identification for both the young
> people and the general Catholic population were not
> issues of sex, birth control, abortion, and the ordination
> of women. Rather, the strongest predictor of Catholic
> behavior and identification was the quality of the Sunday
> sermon preached in the respondent's parish Church.
> (*American Catholics Since the Council*)

The identity crisis of today's Catholic priest is one that
severely affects vocations to the priesthood. There are many
reasons for the decline in vocations. However, the overriding
factor is the priest himself. Again, to quote Father Greeley:

> . . . The most serious obstacle to increasing the number of
> priestly vocations still seems to be the lack of encourage-
> ment which young men ought to receive from priests
> themselves . . . the principle obstacle to the recruitment

of priests is the lack of enthusiasm for such recruitment
among priests themselves . . . In the absence of more
enthusiasm for vocations in the priesthood, the problem
of diminishing numbers of priests will be insoluble.
(*American Catholics Since the Council*)

What is it that occasions such lack of enthusiasm? Many
priests simply (and tragically) do not appreciate the importance of what they do. The crisis of confidence and enthusiasm
is a crisis of not experiencing priestly ministry in a positive
manner. Therefore, if priests have lost confidence in their
work, they are not likely to encourage others to become priests.
The problem is not with the role of the priesthood, but with the
priests' perception and evaluation of their priestly ministry.
Priests remain important to the laity. Sadly, the priestly
ministry has not remained important to priests. The critical
issue of priestly self-perception should not be minimized.
However, we should view our present priestly crisis in light of
Paul's beautiful farewell message to Timothy:

> In the presence of God and of Christ Jesus, who is coming
> to judge the living and the dead, and by his appearing in
> his kingly power, I charge you to preach the word, to stay
> with this task whether convenient or inconvenient —
> correcting, reproving, appealing — constantly teaching
> and never losing patience . . . I for my part am already
> being poured out like a libation. The time of my dissolu-
> tion is near. I have fought the good fight, I have finished
> the race, I have kept the faith. (2 Tm 4:1-2, 6-7)

The concluding chapter will explore the development of
liberation theology in terms of the pastoral mission of the
Church. This exploration of liberation themes will be conducted *within* the tradition of the Catholic Church. At times,
we will be critical of certain variations of liberation theology.
Such a critical stance is done with the hope of furthering the
cause of justice matured by love; the need to affirm the dignity
of the human person as an image of God; and the goal of true
liberation as reconciliation. Above all, we want to understand
liberation within the preaching of the Kingdom of God. The

liberation for which we yearn is a promise and a hope. No
specific political program or human institution can bring about
perfect peace, justice, and freedom. There is about all of our
working for justice a provisional quality and a prudent awareness of the incompleteness of our efforts. The words of
Reinhold Niebuhr are most appropriate:

> Nothing that is worth doing can be achieved in our
> lifetime; therefore we must be saved by hope. Nothing
> which is true or beautiful or good makes complete sense
> in any immediate context of history; therefore we must be
> saved by faith. Nothing we do, however virtuous, can be
> accomplished alone; therefore we are saved by love. No
> virtuous act is quite as virtuous from our standpoint.
> Therefore we must be saved by the final form of love
> which is forgiveness.

Before focusing on the various pastoral concerns which
claim our attention in this book, a most necessary word of
gratitude must be spoken. My association with Alba House has
been a sheer joy. Fathers Timothy and Edmund have been
most encouraging and they do their priestly ministry with great
zeal and enthusiasm. Father Victor is an old friend and was my
first contact with the Society of Saint Paul when he served as
editor of *Pastoral Life*. I am grateful to the Monks of Saint
Joseph Abbey who continue to make welcome this diocesan
priest in the true spirit of Saint Benedict. I have been blessed
with students who ask questions and continue to remind me of
how much I don't know! I hope they will read this book, point out
its shortcomings, and help me to write a better one next time.

William F. Maestri
Saint Joseph Abbey
Saint Benedict, Louisiana

"One possesses the Holy Spirit in the measure
that one loves the Church of Christ."
— *Saint Augustine*

PAUL'S PASTORAL VISION

I

THE PASTORAL LETTERS OF PAUL:
An Overview

The Catholic Church is a pastoral Church. In every aspect of Church life, the pastoral dimension must be present and celebrated. The three fundamental aspects of Church life — creed/belief, code/conduct, and cult/worship — must be pastoral, that is, they must be about bringing Christ to the human family and the human family to Christ. This pastoral mission of the Church comes from Jesus Christ and was present at the beginning:

> Then he opened their minds to understand the Scriptures, and said to them, "Thus it is written, that the Christ should suffer and on the third day rise from the dead, and that repentance and forgiveness of sins should be preached in his name to all nations, beginning from Jerusalem. You are my witnesses of these things." (Lk 24:45-48)

In Acts, we are presented with the Ascension of Jesus and his commission to the disciples, "You shall receive power when the Holy Spirit has come upon you; and you shall be my witnesses in Jerusalem and in all Judea and Samaria and to the ends of the earth" (Ac 1:8).

The temptation is always present to withdraw from the

world and passively wait for Jesus to return. The temptation is to remain behind closed doors out of fear or to strike a triumphal stance of superiority. The words of the men in white robes are as important today as they were on that Ascension day. "Men of Galilee, why do you stand looking into the skies? This Jesus, who was taken up from you into heaven, will come in the same way as you saw him go into heaven" (Ac 1:11). The pastoral Church of Jesus Christ must continually listen for the sound of the mighty rush of the Spirit and must continually look for that fire which renews our hearts and the face of the earth. The pastoral Church is a Church of Pentecost and a community of hope which proclaims the death and resurrection of the Lord until he comes again.

To call the Church of Jesus Christ a pastoral Church (which is more than the Catholic Church) is to remember an essential dimension of the Church's identity. As mentioned above, this pastoral dimension was present at the beginning. This means that we can (and must) look into our past for guidance and hope. We can look to our ancestors in faith, as in a distant mirror, in order to better see what we are about today and what we can be tomorrow. The befriending of our biblical tradition is no small achievement in an age which celebrates the now and only looks back in anger at yesterday. Such a befriending does not turn the Scriptures or any one historical moment of the Church's reflection into a hitching-post. Rather, we are provided with valuable models and insights concerning pastoral practice. James M. Gustafson has written about befriending our biblical tradition and the subsequent models they offer:

> Paradigms are basic models of a vision of life, and of the practice of life, from which flow certain consistent attitudes, outlooks . . . rules or norms of behavior, and specific actions . . . The paradigm *in*forms and *in*fluences the life of the community and its members as they become what they are under their own circumstances. (*The Relation of the Gospels to the Moral Life*)

We cannot state strongly enough that the befriending of our biblical tradition is not a call to biblical fundamentalism or literalism. Rather, it is a sign of maturity, in that, like the prudent steward, we are able to draw new insights from perennial treasures. The Spanish-American philosopher, George Santayana, wrote of three stages in the life of the mind. The first stage finds it difficult to concentrate and is often distracted by the shallow and flashy. The second stage is one of maturity which is characterized by the ability to synthesize the wisdom of the past with the insights of the present. The final stage is one of exhaustion and a tiring, mindless, repetition of the past. The challenge for the individual and the community is to change often (Cardinal Newman). In the words of Santayana:

> In a moving world re-adaptation is the price of longevity. The hard shell, far from protecting the vital principle, condemns it to die down slowly and be gradually chilled; immortality is such a case must have been secured earlier, by giving birth to a generation plastic to the contemporary world and able to retain its lessons. Thus old age is as forgetful as youth, and more incorrigible; it displays the same inattentiveness to conditions; its memory becomes self-repeating and degenerates into an instinctive reaction, like a bird's chirp. (*The Life of Reason*)

The community of faith we call the Church must possess that maturity which allows for a befriending of the past while exhibiting a "plasticity and fertile re-adaptation." Each generation of Christians is called to give "birth to a generation plastic to the contemporary world and able to retain its lessons." Such a calling and hope are not grounded in our all too human achievements but in the abiding presence of the Paraclete who guides us in the way of all truth (Jn 16:13).

Throughout this book, we will be exploring some of our pressing pastoral concerns through the "distant mirror" of Paul's Pastoral Letters. Again, we are not interested in a nostalgic return to some golden age which in reality never existed. We want to be mature enough, in Santayana's use of the term, to learn the lessons of the past while being plastic enough to respond to the Spirit who blows where it wills. With this in mind, we now turn our attention to the Pastoral Letters of the Apostle Paul.

General Overview

The Pastoral Letters were written, in that beautiful Jewish phrase, "between the evenings." The Apostolic age was waning and a new epoch was about to be born. As with all periods of transition, there was a certain amount of anxiety and uncertainty. The old forms and structures were being called into question. What would take their place had not yet appeared. Naturally, there were voices which demanded an "advance to the past" and a nostalgic yearning for that "old time religion." Others were enthusiastic about the novel and wanted to plunge forward into tomorrow. Change had not occurred fast enough. The challenge was clear enough: to effect a prudent change which would be respectful of the Apostolic teaching while at the same time following the Holy Spirit with courage. The challenge was also structural. New challenges and opportunities faced the early Church for which past structures and organization would be inadequate. The answer did not lie with an absence of structure, but a structure that would be respectful of persons and serve as a means for bringing members closer to Christ. Finally the Church would need to develop a new way of thinking about the qualities for leadership. The Church was expanding and becoming more visible in the world. Yet great care must be taken so that the community did not become of the world. Pastoral leadership must provide this delicate balance and moral example.

The Catholic Church of today can see much of itself in these Pastoral Letters. In the years following the Second Vatican Council, we have experienced our own "between the evenings." The past 25 years have been times of enormous change coupled with confusion, anxiety, and excess. Yet this period has also been a time of the Spirit. New structures, along with new forms of worship, have been developed. The laity have been encouraged to take a more active role in parish life. There has been a virtual explosion of courses and books dealing with the Bible.

The moral life has come to be seen as something more than obeying rules and regulations. A greater emphasis has been placed on conversion and growth in the spiritual life. All of these and many more have been exciting and, at the same time, also evidenced their share of weaknesses. This was true in the time of Paul, it is true in our time, and it will continue to be true until Christ comes again in glory.

The Pastoral Letters are I and II Timothy and Titus. They are different from the rest of the letters of Paul. Along with the letter to Philemon, the Pastoral Letters were addressed to individuals. The other letters of Paul were addressed to churches. Simply because they were sent to individuals, we should not conclude that they have no relevance for the Church as a whole. These personal letters are pastoral, that is, they raise some of the more pressing challenges and opportunities confronting the Church in every age: leadership in the Church; the need to remain faithful to Apostolic teaching; the proper attention to be shown to the ministries of teaching and preaching; the need for the community of faith to grow in the moral and spiritual life; and the crucial need to train future leaders for the community.

Before we explore in some detail the various concerns raised in the Pastoral Letters, we will consider the following by way of general background and introduction: date of composition and authorship; organization of each letter; and various pastoral themes raised in each letter.

Date of Composition and Authorship

Biblical scholars are not in agreement as to the date of composition of the Pastoral Letters as well as the actual authorship of each letter. For those scholars who hold that the

Apostle Paul wrote the Pastorals, the date of composition would be between 60 and 64 A.D. Scholars who contend that Paul did not write these letters place the composition date much later, possibly as late as 115 A.D. However, the most probable date of composition for those who reject these as being from the pen of Paul is 90 A.D.

Scholars make their determination as to the authorship of the books in the Bible on the basis of internal and external evidence.

Internal evidence includes tone, style, structure, vocabulary, and general theological message in light of other accepted writings by a particular author. Those scholars who hold to Pauline authorship base their claims on the following:

1. Even though the vocabulary and style of the Pastoral Letters are unlike those in other Pauline letters, this does not necessarily deny authorship to Paul. Different circumstances require a different type of style and vocabulary. In writing to various churches, Paul used one style. In writing to individuals, he used another. Furthermore, the differences in style and vocabulary are exaggerated. This is all much ado about nothing.

2. The Pastoral Letters do not contain a Church structure reflective of the second century. The Pastorals reflect a structure associated with the middle of the first century. There is no mention of a hierarchy and its corresponding clear separation of duties and powers. For example, we do not read, as we do with the epistles of Ignatius of Antioch in the second century, of a community with its own bishop, priests, and deacons. The Pastoral Letters are more reflective of the organizational realities present in New Testament times.

3. The Pastorals do mention that threat posed by false teachers. However, those who hold for Pauline authorship of the Pastorals do not associate these dangerous teachers with the Gnosticism of the second century. Rather, they contend that such Gnostic teachers were really Jewish and reflective of the first century. The Gnosticism with which the Pastorals were contending concerned the Mosaic Law. Such Jewish

Gnosticism taught that there was a dualism between spirit and the material creation; that the Parousia had already come; that there was a need to strictly observe all dietary laws so as to remain pure; and that there must be a prohibition against marriage. All these concerns were addressed by Paul in his Pastoral Letters, or so scholars who hold for Pauline authorship contend.

The external evidence often mentioned to support Pauline authorship includes the following: early Church writers such as Irenaeus, Barnabas, Ignatius, Polycarp, and Clement made mention of these letters as having been written by Paul. Those who raised early doubts about their authenticity as Pauline were accused of not accepting the teaching contained in the letters. At least such a charge is advanced in the writings of Jerome and Tertullian.

Biblical scholars who question the Pauline authorship of the Pastoral Letters do so on the following grounds: internally, the language, style, and tone are very different from Paul's letters to the churches. In addition to the questions of vocabulary and literary style, scholars also associate the false teachings of the Pastorals with the Gnosticism of the second century. The organizational structures of the community reflected in these letters are indicative of the second century and not the first.

When all is written, and the scholarly dust has settled, we must ask: Did Paul write the Pastorals or not? And a second question arises: If Paul did not write them, does that mean that they have no value for the Christian and the faith community?

The consensus of scholarly opinion concerning Pauline authorship of the Pastorals would be that Paul did not write the letters himself. However, we must be quick to mention a crucial aspect of authorship present in Paul's time, but not operative in ours. Namely, that it was not uncommon for a disciple of a famous teacher to sign the teacher's name to a work which the disciple had written. This was not done in order to deceive but out of respect and gratitude. The goal of the disciple was to "put on the mind" of the teacher. The disciple wanted to study under a certain teacher so that he could become like the teacher. Imitation was the sincerest form of flattery. Hence, it is quite possible that one of Paul's disciples wrote these letters in his name. A disciple who knew the mind of Paul would have felt quite comfortable in doing such a thing.

To our second question, do the letters, if they were not from the hand of Paul, possess any value for the Christian and the community of faith, William Barclay has supplied the best answer:

> In the Pastoral Epistles we are still hearing the voice of Paul, and often hearing it with a unique personal intimacy; but we think that the form of the letters is due to a Christian teacher who summoned the help of Paul when the Church of the day needed the guidance which only he could give.

These wise words of Barclay remind us of several important things.

First, a living tradition is a priceless treasure. Though Paul had died, his vision and voice continued to be present in the community, building up the Body of Christ. It is the wise community which knows how to value its past so as to enrich its present and provide hope for the future.

Second, the good teacher is able to creatively and faithfully apply the insights of the past to current needs. Such a teacher does not view the tradition as a hitching-post but rather as a sign-post. The tradition is living and most vibrant when it points to the God who lives and cares for us.

Third, the inspiring work of the Holy Spirit continues through the generations and is not frozen in time. The Spirit continues to be with the community and its leaders. Each generation of Christians must answer old questions ("Who do people say that I am?" "Who do you say that I am?" "What do you seek?" "What must I do to gain eternal life?") and face new challenges (the arms race in the nuclear age; the bio-medical revolution; the role of women in the Church). We do not face such challenges without resources and the abiding presence of the Paraclete. We can learn much from this unknown disciple of Paul as he applied his teacher's love for Jesus Christ to new challenges. No doubt the Spirit was at work in him and in the community. So it is in our own day. Leaders, teachers, and the community as a whole must look to the resources of our blessed tradition, all the while being prayerfully attentive to the promptings of the Spirit today.

We shall now turn our attention to the Pastoral Letters themselves in terms of their organization and the major themes raised in each letter. Robert J. Karris, O.F.M., in his excellent commentary (*The Pastoral Epistles*, volume 17 of the New Testament Message series by Michael Glazier, Inc.), suggests that, in discussing the Pastorals, we begin with II Timothy and then proceed to I Timothy and Titus. His suggestion is a sound one, for the order of the letters in the Bible is based on the length, longest (I Timothy) to shortest (Titus); the letters are written at the same time; and there is no mention in the letters themselves that one letter be read prior to another. Hence, we are at liberty to read them in an alternate order. And Karris suggests that we read them in his suggested order because II Timothy places such "great emphasis on the person and image of Paul." The Pastoral Letters raise a number of crucial pastoral concerns but these concerns can never be separated from the Apostle and Pastor who is present on each page. If Emerson is correct that the measure of an institution is the shadow cast by great individuals, then we can say that the Pastorals are to be measured by the shadow of the great pastor Paul.

Organization and Themes: II Timothy

There are a number of ways to organize or outline the Second Letter to Timothy. Naturally, the one who wrote this letter did not do so in terms of chapter and verse. The placing of the Scriptures in chapter and verse is a way of helping us to organize and better understand God's word. For our purposes, the following outline is offered:

OUTLINE

1:1-2   Paul sends a communication to Timothy with love and a prayer for God's mercy and peace in Christ Jesus.

1:3-4:8   The body of the letter, which exhorts faithfulness to the Gospel and the need to be on guard against the teachings of a false Gospel.

4:9-22   The letter closes with some news about Paul and his fellow workers in the Gospel. There is mention of Paul being hurt by Alexander the coppersmith, but the grace of God saw Paul through. Timothy must keep up the sound preaching. Finally, the letter ends with a greeting to some friends and a prayer for the grace and peace of the Lord to abide.

Within the above outline, there are a number of important themes which deserve brief mention.

1. *The Foundation of Ministry.* Ours is an age which likes to take the measure of things. We have come to believe that in the quantity is the quality; bigger is better. The successful businessman is known by the abundance of his possessions and the net worth of his buildings. *Forbes* magazine each year crowns "the richest person" in the world. The intelligent person is measured by an IQ score, a GPA, or a college entrance examination. The successful pastor is one who exhibits the "edifice complex." He builds great buildings and preaches to large crowds. Everyone speaks well of him. Yet 2 Timothy 1:6-18 challenges the whole quest for success in terms of the world's agenda.

The successful pastor is the *faithful* pastor. And the foundation of the pastoral ministry is the Holy Spirit. Fidelity requires moral courage. There are many temptations to follow alternate Gospels and substitute lords. Even if all should decide to forsake the company of the pastor, the Gospel of Jesus Christ must be preached. This Gospel is no mere human invention. It is the very power of God to save our souls. We are not allowed to "play fast and loose" with its message of forgiveness and hope. To be faithful to the Gospel brings one face to face with the "cost of discipleship." Paul knew this cost well:

> In the service of this Gospel I have been appointed preacher and apostle and teacher, and for its sake I undergo present hardships. But I am not ashamed, for I know him in whom I have believed, and I am confident that he is able to guard what has been entrusted to me until that Day. (2 Tm 1:11-12)

What is the Gospel which Paul had preached with great power and followed with such great fidelity? The Gospel is beautifully captured by Paul in these few verses:

> God has saved us and has called us to his holy life. Not because of any merit of ours but according to his own design — the grace held over to us in Christ Jesus before the world began but now made manifest through the appearance of our Savior. He has robbed death of its power and has brought life and immortality into clear light through the Gospel. (2 Tm 1:9-10)

To deviate from this good news is to abandon "sound teaching" in favor of myths and fables. This good news and the ministry are not human achievements but pure gifts of God's unbounded love for us. The gifts of Gospel and ministry exact a price since no disciple is above the Master. Yet the same Father whose Spirit strengthened Jesus will do the same for the "little flock" which remains in the world.

    2. *Sound Teaching.* Teaching is more than the presentation of facts and information. Teaching always reveals the character of the teacher. The ministry of teaching the Gospel requires that the good news become visible in the life of the teacher (and preacher). Sound teaching also calls for sound living. Hence, Paul could say to Timothy, "Take as a model of sound teaching what you have heard me say, in faith and love in Christ Jesus" (2 Tm 1:13). And again, Paul exhorted Timothy:

> You have followed closely my teaching and my conduct.
> You have observed my resolution, fidelity, patience,
> love, and endurance, through persecution and sufferings
> . . . You, for your part, must remain faithful to what you
> have learned and believed, because you know who your
> teachers were. (2 Tm 3:10-11, 14)

These words of Paul are not words of empty boasting or
pride. Rather, Paul could offer his life as an example *because
of what God had done for and through him in the Spirit of Jesus.*
Paul's life and ministry were living testimony to others of
amazing grace.

Paul saw an essential connection between false teaching
and preaching and a subsequent decline of morality in the
community. At work were those who were teaching a different
Gospel. The false teachers at Ephesus (2 Tm 2:14-26) were
preaching that the resurrection had already occurred. The
Parousia had been fully realized. There was no bodily resurrection. Hence, once we received the waters of baptism, the
fullness of new life would be ours for all eternity. Such a
doctrine was aimed at making the teaching about resurrection
more acceptable to the Gentiles. In the name of winning over
converts and not offending the sensibilities of anyone, the
Gospel can be made to order. The end justifies the means.
Unfortunately, we are presented with a classic example of the
doctrine of unintended consequences. That is, the unforeseen
and complete opposite of what was expected or hoped for
happened. Instead of a spiritual rebirth, there was a general
decline in the moral life of the community. In the theology of
today, without a true orthodoxy, there can be no authentic
orthopraxis. Ideas still matter and serve as the parents of our
deeds. In the words of Paul:

> Men will be lovers of self and of money, proud, arrogant,
> abusive, disobedient to their parents, ungrateful, pro-
> fane, inhuman . . . hating the good . . . For the time will
> come when people will not tolerate sound doctrine, but

. . . will surround themselves with teachers who tickle their ears. They will stop listening to the truth and will wander off to fables. (2 Tm 3:2-3; 4:3-4)

3. *Comfort My Minister.* The call to ministry is anything but a call to be excused from this all too human condition. The minister is made of clay and is an earthen vessel. The rush of the Spirit on the anointing with oils does not make one immune from discouragement, fear, uncertainty, and sin. In fact, to be a minister of the Gospel is an invitation to be drawn more deeply into this poor flesh which is also meant for glory. We must truly become "wounded healers." It is a dangerous minister (and a tragic ministry) who fails to allow the words and worship to become flesh. In the twelfth chapter of John's Gospel, we are told that some Greeks came looking for Jesus. They approached Philip with this request, "Sir, we would like to see Jesus." Here is the essence of the pastoral ministry — allowing others to see Jesus. Ministry is allowing and empowering others to see Jesus in their lives; in the Scriptures which can inflame their hearts; in the Eucharist which can nourish their deepest hungers; in the preached word which can comfort and challenge; and to see Jesus at work in the pastor. The outstanding Jesuit theologian and preacher, Walter J. Burghardt, S.J., has written:

> Ultimately, *I* am the word, the word that is heard. And I say it fearfully — it is not a clever rhetorician the people need, but a holy homilist. Holy in what sense? Because aware that I am only *a* word, not *the* word: If God does not speak through me, I am "a noisy gong, a clanging cymbal" (1 Cor 13:1). Because my homily is a prayer: in preparation and pulpit, I stand before God in praise of Him, not of my own rhetorical perfection. Because aware of my own weakness: I too need the word I preach. I too need forgiveness, I too am vulnerable, I am a *wounded* healer. Because, like my hearers, I too ceaselessly murmur, "I believe, Lord, help my unbelief." Because I am in love with the things of God, with the people of God,

with God himself. Because the hungers of God's family
are my hungers: when they bleed, I weep. Unless some of
this breaks through, the word may indeed be proclaimed,
but it will hardly be heard. (*Preaching: The Art and the
Craft*)

The Apostle Paul knew first hand that ministry is more
than worldly wisdom and great signs. The ministry of the
Gospel requires a faithful teaching and preaching so

that Christ may live in your hearts through faith, and
then, planted in love and built on love, you will with all
the saints have strength to grasp the breadth and the
length, the height and the depth; until knowing the love of
Christ, which is beyond all knowledge, you are filled with
the utter fullness of God. (Ep 3:17-19)

Yet even with the message of this great mystery of God's
unbounded love comes rejection and hostility. Yet even in the
face of the faithful preaching and teaching there is still
apostasy. Yet even with sound teaching and leaders who
imitate Christ there are still those who follow the ways of sin.
What is the pastor to do?
The pastor feels the hurts, temptations, and loneliness of
his community. The pastor is tempted to self-doubt and feelings of inadequacy. However, the pastor must keep on keeping
on. The good pastor does not deny these human feelings, but
hands them over to the God who heals and strengthens. The
good pastor is faithful. And the faithful pastor is a person of
love in imitation of the One who loved us till the end and into a
new beginning. There is nothing to be gained by engaging in
useless debate. There is even less to be gained by condemning
people and trading angry insults. The good pastor is a person
who is constant in message and manner; in preaching the
Gospel and in loving as Jesus showed us how to love. The
presence of the Spirit enables the minister to remain constant
in teaching and character. Hardships and opposition are to be
expected, but the joy of the Gospel is greater still. Concerning

this need for ministerial constancy, Stanley Hauerwas has written with great insight:

> I can think of no virtue more necessary to the ministry today than constancy. Without steadfastness to self and to one's task I do not see how the ministry can be sustained. Without constancy the minister is tempted to abandon the Church to the ever present temptation of unbelief and unbelief's more powerful ally, sentimentality . . . Constancy, moreover, suggests the kind of character required by the nature of the ministerial office . . . it is required of those in ministry to be constant in all that they are and do . . . that persons in the ministry will be faithful to their calling even if such faithfulness risks unpopularity . . . for the Church itself must be comprised of people who require their ministry to do the unpopular thing. A ministry of character is only possible if we are a people of character. ("Clerical Character: Reflecting on Ministerial Morality," *Word & World*, Spring, 1986.)

The Second Letter to Timothy is a word of comfort. It is a word of recognition that pastoral ministry will involve hardships and, at times, one will be a lonely voice crying in the wilderness. Yet one is never really alone, for the Spirit continues to abide and strengthen one in preaching the word "in season and out of season . . . unfailing in patience and in teaching" (2 Tm 4:2). The letter is a word of fellowship between those who accept the invitation of Jesus to proclaim the good news of salvation. There is the recognition that ministers of the Gospel must support, comfort, and encourage one another. Ministry cannot be romanticized and sentimentalized into a kind of "lion in winter" model. The ministry of the Gospel is entrusted to a community and from that community of faith, God raises up those who will preach the good news. And finally, comfort comes to those who are faithful (constant) in their ministry. Paul, near the end of his life and his ministry, left a touching last testimony to Timothy:

> For I am already on the point of being sacrificed; the time for my departure has come. I have fought the good fight, I have finished the race, I have kept the faith. Henceforth, there is laid up for me the crown of righteousness, which the Lord, the righteous judge, will award to me that Day, and not only to me but also to all who have longed for his appearing. (2 Tm 4:6-8)

The ultimate comfort does not come from the community, one's fellow ministers, or even the ministry itself. The ultimate comfort comes from God who alone is just and righteous. Human comfort has its limits and the heart is very fickle. Human standards of justice are inadequate at best. It is God alone who truly rewards us according to our needs. What is crucial is that our name is written in the book of life.

Organization and Themes: I Timothy

Once again, there are a number of ways to organize this Pastoral Letter. Our outline will highlight the major themes of the letter. We shall then offer a brief word about its major pastoral themes.

OUTLINE

1:1-2   Paul sends a communication to Timothy whom Paul considers to be a "true child in faith."

1:3-6:19 The body of the letter, which concerns itself with the following:
The struggle against false teachers (1:3-20);
The organization of the Church along with the requirements for those who hold office in the Church (2:1-3:16);
The expectations placed on Timothy as a pastoral leader of the community of faith (4:12-6:2); and
The need for Timothy to remain faithful to sound teaching and preaching against the heretics (6:3-19).

6:20-21   The letter closes with a final warning against the false teachers and prayers for Timothy.

A number of important pastoral issues are raised in this letter. In subsequent chapters, we will develop these issues. For now, a brief word about three major themes is in order.

1. *Sound Teaching.* The Pastoral Letters can trouble a comfortable mind which has come of age nurtured on a live and let live philosophy. In the much uncelebrated *The Closing of the American Mind* (something which is by no means confined to the American experience), Professor Allan Bloom writes:

> There is one thing a professor can be absolutely certain of: almost every student entering the university believes or says he believes that truth is relative . . . The danger they have been taught to fear from absolutism is not error but intolerance. Relativism is necessary to openness; and this is the virtue, the only virtue, which all primary education for more than fifty years has dedicated itself to inculcating. Openness . . . the great insight of our times. The true believer is the real danger . . . There is no enemy other than the man who is not open to everything.

Professor Bloom goes on to wonder if such a mind set is capable of possessing a vision of the common good; sharing social goals; and joining in establishing democratic social control. Bloom leaves little doubt that such a task is becoming increasingly difficult. Similar concerns were raised by the Pastor Paul writing to Timothy. The "closing of the Christian soul" was very much a concern of Paul. Sound teaching and preaching are all the more necessary given the rise of doctrines which challenge the Gospel of Jesus Christ. Paul was not opposed to an openness which truly seeks to know Christ and the power flowing from his resurrection. However, there was, and is, an openness of indifference which rejects the notion of truth as an objective reality. Truth is nothing more or less than what pleases me and makes me comfortable. About such a "truth" there can be no real argument. Each ends up doing his own thing and believing his own dogma. Again the words of Professor Bloom are worthy of consideration:

> Openness, as currently conceived, is a way of making surrender to whatever is most powerful, or worship of vulgar success, look principled. It is historicism's ruse to remove all resistance to history, which in our day means public opinion, a day when public opinion already rules . . . True openness is the accompaniment of the desire to know, hence of the awareness of ignorance. To deny the possibility of knowing good and bad is to suppress true openness. (*The Closing of the American Mind*)

William Barclay has written with great insight about the New Testament. He was a man of great intellectual abilities and a deep spiritual love for the word of God. Barclay, in his writings on the Pastoral Letters, makes it clear that Paul believed that various false teachings were extremely dangerous for the faith of the community. The centrality of Jesus for our salvation was under attack. In addition, some members of the community were becoming involved with idle speculations and wasting time on fables. All this detracted from the essential work of the Gospel. The faith life of the community could not afford such teachings to go unchallenged because of the serious consequences for the moral life. Factionalism and elitism would develop and replace love with anger, bitterness, and competition. At issue was the truth of the Gospel and the eternal disposition of one's soul.

We need to make a careful distinction between responsible and irresponsible dissent. A person can dissent from an authentic teaching in a responsible way. He makes a genuine effort to understand the orthodox position. He prayerfully considers and reconsiders his position. He respectfully states his position in love, but in conscience must believe as he does. There is no sense of joy or celebrity in the dissent. There is a real sense of loss and a severe rupture in the relationship. This is not the kind of dissent which concerned Paul. Paul contended with those forms of dissent which were self-serving and led the community away from the Gospel. In 1 Tm 1:3-7, Paul provided us with a list of characteristics which are associated with irresponsible dissent and a corresponding set of characteristics exhibited by the faithful teacher.

IRRESPONSIBLE DISSENT	FAITHFUL TEACHER
1. There is a strong desire for idle speculations for their own sake.	1. The faithful teacher hands on the authentic Gospel of Jesus. Novelty is not to be equated with truth.
2. A living faith based on knowledge of Jesus Christ is rejected in the name of an intellectual knowing of various myths and fables.	2. A love which imitates the example given by Jesus is the driving force of all Gospel teaching. Without love, we become filled with pride and arrogance.
3. The command of Jesus to love is ignored in favor of vain discussions. The Christian life becomes one of words over deeds.	3. The character of the faithful teacher is one of purity and sincerity. Only one thing is willed — to follow Jesus in spirit and truth.
4. There is an arrogance and self-righteousness which leads to a rejection of all who do not agree with one's teachings.	4. God's many gifts are used well. That is, time is not wasted in idle speculation. Much work is to be done while it is still light.
5. There is an absence of real openness to truth. Knowledge about the Gospel is secondary to the defense of one's own insights and teachings.	5. The faithful teacher is a person of humility. One is preaching not oneself but the Gospel of Jesus.

2. *Sound Character.* The message of Jesus Christ, crucified and risen, is entrusted to vessels of clay. Yet within us poor human vessels is "that transcendent power which belongs to God" (2 Cor 4:7). Equally important as purity of doctrine is the need for the pastor to be a person above

reproach. Paul made it abundantly clear what character qualities are to be found in the pastor: he must be a person of
temperate desires; prudent; a good teacher who also provides a
good moral example; a person of reconciliation; and a person
who knows that the real riches are found in the Gospel and not
in the currency of this world. Throughout the Pastoral Letters,
there is a crucial, but too often overlooked, connection between the minister's character and the office to which he is
called. In an age in which we see more and more so-called
"ministerial misconduct" (in a less kind age we might call it
sin!), the need for people of character is crucial. We need to
ask what kind of person is coming before us claiming that God
has called him to serve as a priest. We need to be ever watchful
of the character of those who are called to serve the Church in
various ministries (music, liturgy, religious education). The
importance of the minister's character is *not* one that can be
formed by a code or a set of professional rules. Rather, we are
interested in the character which is formed in a community of
the Gospel. The person called to public service on behalf of the
community must be one who gives public witness to those
virtues (righteousness, godliness, faith, love, steadfastness,
and gentleness) which let all know that we are his disciples.

Paul called Timothy a "man of God." What finer words
could be said of a minister of the Gospel? Paul reminded
Timothy of his dignity and the ultimate source of his ministry.
To call Timothy a man of God was not to provide him with a title
for boasting or privilege. Rather, this was a call and a
challenge to be of service to the community. Such service
comes by faithfully preaching the Gospel; teaching the truths
necessary for salvation; and living a life which inspires others
to love Jesus and their neighbors. The character of the pastoral
minister must be such that he can be God's man and the man
for others with fidelity and moral courage.

3. *Sound Organization.* The mention of Church organization and structure is bound to evoke strong opinions. One
extreme holds that the Church structure mentioned in the New
Testament (or some other golden age of one's choosing) cannot

be changed but must be copied from one generation to the next until Christ comes again. The opposite extreme advocates the removal of all structure and hierarchy. Organization produces routine and routine tames the spirit. That organization leads best which organizes least. Needless to say, both of these extremes lack the virtue of prudence. The first position does not take seriously the provisional nature of every Church structure in light of the Kingdom. And the second fails to take seriously the human need to organize what is most important for our life together.

Ecclesiologist Father Avery Dulles, S.J. wisely rejects both of the above-mentioned positions. Father Dulles, in light of a prudent reading of the signs of the times, advances five trends which are presently at work in contemporary Church structures:

1. The Catholic Church is not immune to the trends of modernization. Modern political thought advocates a greater degree of participation and equality among members. Also, modern thought views authority in a more functional and less ceremonial way. Such modernizing trends can be a real opportunity for the Church to respond to the needs of the time. Within the Church's tradition and biblical witness is the model of authority as service. The modernizing trend will also be a challenge. The Church will need to blend equality of participation with the evangelical idea that a pastoral office is a call from God.

2. Denominational divisions continue to exist but progress has been made toward a responsible unity of the Christian Church. Church leaders will be challenged to find creative ways to continue and enrich the dialogue. Between now and the time when "all will be one," structures and organization should be developed so that the areas of agreement can be celebrated and the areas of disagreement addressed.

3. In addition to the modernizing trends of equality and democratic participation, we also have witnessed the rise of pluralism. Such a pluralism has been at work in terms of decentralization. The local levels of the universal Church have

been given greater autonomy and an increased sense of responsibility for the faith life of the community. Again, a prudent balance must be struck between a responsible local autonomy and a fidelity to the universal Church in Rome. There is an opportunity to develop structures which draw on the insights and gifts of the local community as well as the faith witness of other Christian denominations.

4. A great deal of thought and prayer must be given to developing structures which are both stable and open to the needs of new generations of Christians. Without stability, we easily conform to the latest cultural dress and fads. Without the ability to adapt and be open to the Spirit, Church structures become monuments to irrelevancy, or worse, they become idols.

5. The Church must come to rely more and more on its ability to persuade and inspire. The days of commanding and condemning have long passed. Those in authority will be about building consensus rather than giving orders. Teaching will be less concerned with external conformity and more with an ongoing transformation of the heart (conversion). To some, this may sound like a loss of power and the Church's becoming an "uncertain trumpet." Yet in reality, this is a growth and maturity into the full stature of Christ. The ability to reason, persuade, and inspire is more respectful of the human person. (For a detailed discussion of the above themes, see the following major works by Avery Dulles, S.J.: *Models of the Church*; *Models of Revelation*; and *A Church to Believe in*.)

In reading the Pastorals (especially 1 Timothy), we are presented with a way of structuring and organizing the faith community. There is no suggestion that this is *the only way*. Clearly, the advice given by the Pastorals to various members of society and Church is limited by culture and history. For example, we read, "Let those who are under the yoke of slavery regard their masters as worthy of all honor, so that the name of God and the teaching may not be defamed" (1 Tm 6:11). Naturally, these words reflect a particular social and historical reality. None of us would advocate the slavery of one human being by another. The word of God comes mediated through the words of human beings who are limited by space, time, and the reality of sin. The Holy Spirit continues to work in our hearts and community and structure. We see through a glass darkly. We live in the hope of a promise that one day we shall know as we are known and we shall see God as he is. Until that time, we prayerfully and prudently make pilgrimage toward the Kingdom of God. Father Avery Dulles deserves the last word:

> Under the leading of the Holy Spirit the images and forms of Christian Life will continue to change, as they have in previous centuries. In a healthy community of faith the production of new myths and symbols goes on apace. The ecclesiologists of the future will no doubt devise new models of thinking about the Church. But what is new in Christianity always grows out of the past and has its roots in Scripture and tradition. On the basis of the relative continuity of the past two thousand years it seems safe to predict that the analogies and paradigms discussed in this book will retain their significance for ecclesiology through many generations yet to come. (*Models of the Church*)

Organization and Themes: Titus

The Letter to Titus completes our general overview of the Pastoral Letters. Once again, we shall present a brief outline of the letter, along with a brief discussion of the major themes. The Letter to Titus raises some of the major pastoral themes already discussed in previous Pastoral Letters. However, there is a great deal of emphasis placed on the role and character of the Christian teacher. The Christian teacher will occupy our attention in a subsequent chapter. The importance of the moral character of the teacher has taken on renewed interest in our own time. The Letter to Titus has much to offer and we have much to learn.

OUTLINE

1:1-4   The letter opens with the name of Paul, identified as
            a "servant of God and an apostle of Jesus Christ."
            Mention is made of the duty to preach and live a
            moral life. Titus and faithful members of the com-
            munity are greeted with the prayer for God's grace
            and peace.

1:5-3:11   The body of the letter is concerned with the need to
            promote sound teaching through the calling of
            teachers who are faithful to the Gospel. The danger
            of false teachers is present. False teachings can be
            overcome by fidelity to the Gospel and love for God's
            truth. The community of faith has a profound role to
            play in promoting the faith.

3:12-15   The letter ends with some personal commissions
            along with greetings and a final blessing.

Titus was not a bishop but a personal representative of
Paul. He was given the responsibility of forming the Church at
Crete and providing sound teaching. The Letter to Titus can be
divided into three major sections. As with the other Pastoral
Letters, we shall offer a brief word about each theme.

1. Throughout the Letter to Titus, holding center stage
are the character and spiritual requirements of the elder of the
community. He must be a man who is blameless and avoids
giving scandal in both his public and private life. He must
shun arrogance and promote humility; he must live gently and
avoid rash anger; and he should not seek those treasures which
pass away but should set his heart on the Kingdom. As
mentioned in the other two Pastoral Letters, the elder

> must hold firm to the sure word as taught, so that he may
> be able to give instruction in sound doctrine and also to
> confute those who contradict it. For there are many
> insubordinate men, empty talkers and deceivers, espe-
> cially the circumcision party; they must be silenced,

since they are upsetting whole families by teaching for
base gain what they have no right to teach. (Tt 1:10-11)

2. How are these false teachings to be silenced? The best
response lies with the public witness given by the community
of faith. And this brings us to our second major theme in Titus.
The Christian life is a shared life lived by believing members
who proclaim Jesus as Lord and who love one another. The
false teachers in the Church at Crete preached a different
Gospel. They called for a return to the Mosaic practices of the
past (circumcision). In effect, they rendered Jesus' death and
resurrection meaningless for salvation. Paul made it clear that
their motive was not an honest pursuit of the truth but simply a
desire for money, popularity, and power. To counteract this
dangerous teaching, the Christian community (especially the
elders) must provide good examples and live a life worthy of
their calling. The fruits of the Christian community (love,
peace, joy, and reconciliation) would provide eloquent
testimony as to who was in the truth.

3. A final theme in Titus follows from the first two,
namely, the distinctiveness of the Christian community. Simply put, the Christian is just not like everyone else. There is
about discipleship a cost which often places one at odds with
the *status quo* and the taken-for-granted views of what is true,
beautiful, and good. The Christian is always a little (sometimes
a lot) alienated from the crowd. The Christian's angle of vision
and core of values reflect the City of God more than the earthly
City of Man. Jesus is Lord and all others who claim our
ultimate allegiance are dismissed as pretenders and false
messiahs.

The Christian lives a new life in Christ. To be in Christ is
to be a new creation-in-process. We are a pilgrim people on
that journey of faith toward that new heavenly Jerusalem. Until
that time when he comes again in glory, the Christian community must remain in the world giving powerful witness to Jesus
as Lord. And this witness is *public*. The world *needs* the public
witness of the Church, for without the Church, the world will

not know its true dignity, destiny, and Lord. The world needs the Church to continually call it to conversion. The world needs to have its illusions of ultimate power shattered by the Lord who alone gives life in abundance. The Church needs the Gospel so that the Church can remain the Church. Without the Gospel, the Church can easily become an end in itself, an idol. The Church never stands above the Gospel but always under and through the good news it proclaims.

The Pastoral Letters are so insistent on sound teaching and overcoming false doctrines because truth is at issue. God's truth in Jesus has been entrusted to the Church and the Church has the privilege and responsibility to "teach what befits sound doctrine" (Tt 2:1). The Pastorals continually remind us that the Gospel is not a cause for boasting or foolish presumption or quietism. Rather the Christian community is always the humble servant of the word which it is called to preach "in season and out of season." The pastoral mission and ministry of teaching and preaching are the great gifts of God's unbounded grace. And that same grace will also be provided so that the good fight of faith can be fought.

A Concluding Word, a Cautionary Word, and a Foreword

This opening chapter has concerned itself with the Pastoral Letters. We have attempted to provide a brief overview of each letter, along with a brief word of explanation regarding the major themes. No attempt has been made to provide a comprehensive or scholarly discussion of the Pastorals. That is beyond the scope of this book and there are many fine commentaries which accomplish those tasks. Rather, we have wanted to provide an overview of the Pastorals so that the reader may move on to the chapters which follow with a sense of the major issues. If one has such a sense or feel for what is at stake, then what follows will make sense as well. Naturally, no overview or commentary can ever take the place of the Letters themselves and the experience of prayerfully reading God's living word.

A cautionary word must be offered at this time. Throughout this book, we will discuss perennial pastoral issues: leadership, tradition, authority, teaching, vocations, and Church mission, to name but a few. Our discussion will be done with the aid of a "distant mirror," namely, the Pastoral Letters attributed to Paul. By looking at our past, we can better understand our present and journey in hope toward the Kingdom of God. The cautionary word is this: *our approach rejects both Catholic fundamentalism and biblical fundamentalism as contrary to the authentic teachings of the Catholic Church.* The words of the National Conference of Catholic Bishops' Ad Hoc Committee on Biblical Fundamentalism are worthy of remembrance:

> Fundamentalism indicates a person's general approach to life which is typified by an unyielding adherence to rigid doctrinal and ideological positions — an approach that affects the individual's social and political attitudes as well as religious ones. Fundamentalism in this sense is found in non-Christian religions and can be doctrinal as well as biblical.

> Biblical fundamentalists are those who present the Bible, God's inspired word, as the only necessary source for teaching about Christ and Christian living . . . The immediate attractions are the ardor of the Christian community and the promises of certitude and of a personal conversion experience to the person of Jesus Christ without the need of Church. As Catholic pastors, however, we note its presentation of the Bible as a single rule for living. According to fundamentalism, the Bible alone is sufficient. There is no place for the universal teaching Church — including its wisdom, its teachings, creeds and other doctrinal formulations, its liturgical and devotional traditions. There is simply no claim to a visible, audible, living, teaching authority binding the individual or the congregations.

> We believe that no Catholic properly catechized in the

faith can long live the Christian life without those elements that are had only in the fullness of Christianity: the
Eucharist and the other six sacraments, the celebration of
the word in the liturgical cycle, the veneration of the
Blessed Mother and the Saints, teaching authority and
history linked to Christ, and the demanding social
doctrine of the Church based on the soundness of all
human life. (*Pastoral Statement for Catholics on Biblical
Fundamentalism*, released September 30, 1987.)

Throughout this book, there will be no suggestion of a
return to some golden age when everything was perfect. No
such age exists. To so suggest that we stop in time is to be
unfaithful to the abiding, guiding presence of the Holy Spirit.
And furthermore, we cannot be forced to choose between
Church or Bible, Scripture or tradition. We have been given
both so that we may continue our sound teaching and faithful
preaching of the Gospel.

With all of the above in mind, we will now turn our
attention to a number of pressing pastoral concerns: leadership, the role of tradition in the faith community, teacher and
teaching, vocation to the ministry, and the global dimension of
pastoral ministry. It is to the first of these concerns — leadership — that we now turn our attention.

II

PASTORAL LEADERSHIP:
To Be Servant of the Servants

Father Andrew Greeley and his associates (Mary Durkin, David Tracy, John Shea, and William McCready), in their excellent book, *Parish, Priest, and People*, tell a "tale of two parishes." The first parish, St. Leo (not the parish's real name) evidences the worst of times: the clergy have been either autocratic priests who do nothing but give orders and expect blind obedience; or the clergy have been the so-called liberal priests who feel the overwhelming need to help the laity "come of age" and be members of the "where it's at" church, whether the laity wants to or not. The results of such "leadership" are predictable: there is a deep sense of alienation and "gathering storms" of division between pew and pulpit.

The giving orders approach is easy enough to deal with — the laity simply ignore the orders. The days of blind obedience and jumping mindlessly through hoops are gone (if they ever really existed). The giving orders model of ministry and Church is based on the premise that the clergy are totally responsible for parish life and possess superior holiness, knowledge, and training. The role of the laity is to listen, pay, and obey. Questions border on rebellion. The laity have little, if anything, to contribute in terms of decision-making. In effect, the parish belongs to the bishop (or housekeeper if there is still one on the premises!). The laity are to be passive receivers of what the priest ministers to them. Like children, the laity are to be seen (in church on Sundays and Holy Days and in line at the confessional) and not heard.

The giving orders approach is not only bad sociology; it is .bad theology. It is bad sociology because it encourages passivity, apathy, alienation, and a general feeling that one does not belong. Such a feeling produces a loss of identity and purpose. The parishioner simply goes through the motions and performs the external routines without any deep or lasting sense of commitment. And why should she? After all, the parish belongs to the pastor. The parish becomes, in the phrase of Father Johannes Metz, a "service station" parish. That is, people go there to get some religion for the week. They fill up on a little Bible; a dash of sermon; a brief moment of prayerful silence; and maybe even receive the Eucharist. Yet too often they go off and promptly forget what they have seen, heard, and received. There is little or no connection between the main aisle of the church and the main street of one's everyday life. As the week unfolds, the spiritual aspects run down to empty and, hence, it is time for another "fill 'er up" at the local church.

The giving orders approach is bad theology. Through baptism, all are called to be servants of the Gospel. The Holy Spirit has been given to each in a variety of ways. St. Paul, writing to the Corinthians, used the analogy (a wonderfully "Catholic thing") of the body (1 Cor 12). There are many individual parts of the human body. All are vital. All are incomplete without the others. All contribute to a whole which is greater than any of the individual parts. Each member plays its part. The danger is always present that the eye will not see the importance of the ear; the ear will fail to hear the contribution of the other members. Great violence and gross distortion are done if one part is allowed to become the whole of the body.

The Christian community is like the body. The Holy Spirit has bestowed a variety of gifts (that much feared word — pluralism). Some members of the community are called to be teachers, healers, workers of miracles, prophets, speakers in tongues, interpreters of tongues, and discerners of spirits. The variety of gifts always contains the risk of division, jealousy, and factionalism. Too often, we equate the word "different" with the words "more and less." My gift is not only different from yours, but mine is more important for the community and hence, yours is less needed. The giving orders approach is fearful of just such a situation. Pluralism of gifts is really a code word for individualism and "do your own thing Catholicism." In order to overcome such a threat, the pastor must reign and give orders. Only in such an arrangement will unity be preserved.

The Apostle Paul, a pastor of note, advocated another way. The forces of division and strife can only be controlled (but will never be eliminated this side of the Kingdom of God) by setting our hearts on the "more excellent way," that is, love. It is the Spirit of Love which opens our hearts, sharpens our vision, and enlightens our mind so that we can experience the one same Spirit at work in each for the good of all. No one's gift is given at the expense of another. Rather, the Spirit's gifts are given to make up what is lacking in each so that we may join together for the glory of God. The Spirit of Love frees us to see what is lacking in our lives so that other Christians may share their gifts. The Spirit of Love frees me to be generous so that I may give what has been given to me for the good of my neighbor. Far from endangering unity, the Spirit of Love builds a unity which is grounded in the creative, abiding presence of Jesus in the Spirit to the glory of the Father.

Paul's use of the analogy of the body, the presence of the Spirit, the abundance of gifts, and the excellence of love can seem to be nothing more than pious talk or the spiritualizing (escape) of very hard human realities. Such is not the case. Even with the giving of gifts, there is a cost to discipleship. Father Karl Rahner, S.J. has written:

> A charism always involves suffering. For it is painful to fulfill the task set by charism, the gift received, and at the same time within the one body to endure the opposition of

another's activity which may in certain circumstances be equally justified. One's own gift is always limited and humbled by another's gift. Sometimes it must wait until it can develop, until its kairos, its hour, has come and that of another has passed or is fading. This painful fact is to be viewed soberly as an inevitable consequence of there being one Church and many gifts . . . The authenticity of a charism, which after all is for the Church and into the Church, not out of her, is shown by the fact that the person so endowed bears humbly and patiently this inevitable sorrow of his charismatic endowment, builds no little chapel for himself inside the Church in order to make things more tolerable, does not become embittered but knows that it is the one Lord who creates a force and resistance to it, the wine of enthusiasm and the water of sobriety in his Church, and has given to none of his servants singly the task of representing him. (*The Spirit in the Church*)

To simply give orders and demand blind obedience from the laity is to deny the vocation of the laity and their dignity as a "chosen race, a royal priesthood, a holy nation, a people he claims for his own to proclaim the glorious works of the One who called you from darkness into his marvelous light" (1 Peter 2:9). All Christians, through baptism, are called to holiness. Hence, leadership in the Church exhibits holiness and calls the community to be holy through sound teaching and effective preaching. The Second Vatican Council, in its document on the laity, clearly indicates that all members of the faith community are called to play an active role:

> Every activity of the Mystical Body with this in view goes by the name of "apostolate"; the Church exercises it through all its members, though in various ways. In fact, the Christian vocation is of its nature, a vocation to the apostolate as well . . . In the Church there is diversity of ministry but unity of mission. (*Decree on the Apostolate of Lay People*)

None of this is said in order to diminish the role of the priest. The distinctive quality of the priest and his leadership are very much needed. What all of this suggests, rather, is the recognition that each person is called in his own way to serve. And this service does not come at the expense of another's but it is a complementary service which builds up the Body of Christ. The harvest continues to remain rich. There continues to remain the need for the community as a whole to do God's work on earth. This is not the "Protestantization" of the Catholic clergy, but the realization that God's generous love raises up countless men and women to do his will. Such is a cause for rejoicing and not consternation.

At the other end of the extreme is the so-called "liberal-enlightened" approach. The operative sociology and theology are equally offensive and ineffective. The "liberal-enlightened" approach shares with the giving orders approach the belief that the laity must be brought up to a certain level — the level of the enlightened clergy. The process is one of "raising consciousness" so that the oppressed and unenlightened can come of age and take charge. The laity really do not know what is good for them or appropriate. The task of the clergy is to remove all the vestiges of a more immature past (all those things associated with an immigrant Church and the days before Vatican II) and replace them with the new theology, spirituality, and new techniques for more effective pastoral practice. The liberal-enlightened advocate gives as many orders as his reactionary counterpart, but does so more subtly. The best approach from this come of age model is this: bring about change but let them think it was their idea. How strange! The task of raising consciousness is achieved at the same time there is a conscious attempt to deceive. Perhaps what really needs to be raised is the *conscience* level of the self-proclaimed leaders (elite).

The liberal-enlightened approach is bad sociology. In the words of Father Andrew Greeley: "When they are not given an opportunity to participate in the reformation of the parish community, they turn off liberal priests who try to force new ideas on them whether they like them or not" (*Parish, Priest, and People*). Once again, this approach does not call for participation. There is often a great deal of talk about liberty, pluralism, and different opinions. Yet there is frequently a very subtle, but definite, pressure to conform to what has been defined as acceptable by the elite. No one wishes to seem unenlightened, lost in a bygone age, or a stumbling block to the Spirit. Hence, one either silently accepts the new socio-religious definition of reality or one simply does not come to the parish any more. The laity vote with their feet. They shop around for a parish which provides a sense of belonging, participation, identity, and a genuine pluralism which honors the many ways we can experience Jesus and proclaim him as Lord.

The liberal-enlightened approach is bad theology. Such an approach is a modern version of Gnosticism. The enlightened clergy (not so much through ordination as by the power of the latest seminar, book, or pastoral technique one has mastered) are in possession of a special saving knowledge. They feel an obligation to share (or force) this special knowledge with the unenlightened. There is a clear separation between those who know and are saved and those who are still in the dark and in need of salvation. However, the New Testament provides us with a clear record of the results of Gnosticism. The community becomes divided and various factions arise. The spirit of fraternal charity is replaced by fear, hatred, and suspicion. One need only read the Letters of John to see the tragedy which results when we fail to love one another as Jesus loved us. "If anyone says, 'I love God,' and hates his brother, he is a liar; for he who does not love his brother whom he has seen, cannot love God whom he has not seen. And this commandment we have from him, that he who loves God should love his brother also" (1 Jn 4:20-21).

Furthermore, the Gnosticism which motivates the liberal-enlightened approach does not see each person as a child of God. Christian theology teaches that each human being is made in the image and called to grow into likeness of God. Our life is not something we earn but that which is given by God out of total love for us. The dignity of the human person is not one that is earned or bestowed by government, university, or saving human insight. The dignity of the human person is an alien dignity, that is, it is bestowed by the loving God in whose image we are wonderfully made. The Psalmist cannot help but be caught up in the grandeur of such a realization:

> When I look at the heavens, the work of thy fingers,
> the moon and the stars which thou hast established;
> what is man that thou art mindful of him,
> and the son of man that thou dost care for him?
> Yet thou hast made him little less than God,
> and dost crown him with glory and honor.
> Thou hast given him dominion over the works of thy hands;
> thou hast put all things under his feet . . .
> O Lord, our Lord, how majestic is thy name in all the earth!
>
> (Ps 8:3-6, 9)

Jesus and Leadership

The tale of the second parish, St. Anne, operates on the model of servant-leadership. Such an approach rejects giving orders as well as manipulating people into enlightened thinking. Rather, this approach is modeled after Jesus and his ministry of leadership.

The Church of Jesus Christ is just that, the Church of Jesus. It is Jesus whom we proclaim as Lord and Savior. It is Jesus whom we acknowledge as the one ultimate source of life eternal. If our proclamations are to be more than well-worn phrases or pious speeches, we must learn to follow him in the way of leadership. Those who are entrusted with the well-being of the faith community must look to him and follow his example. On the night before he died, Jesus gave the disciples an example of what it meant to be a real teacher, lord, and leader. The leader must be the best footwasher in the community! "If you know these things, blessed are you if you do them" (Jn 13:17).

The Gospels provide us with a number of important episodes in the ministry of Jesus which highlight key aspects of leadership. In calling attention to these examples, we are at the same time rejecting a fundamentalist approach which calls for an uncritical application of the Scriptures. We want rather to learn from Jesus' ministry so that we may continue to proclaim the Gospel in spirit and truth in our time.

1. Leadership requires both the words (Lk 22:14-30) and deeds (Jn 13:1-17) of service. To the contemporary mind, the notions of leadership and service do not mix. Leadership is bold and decisive. Leadership is not allowed the luxury of self-doubt and indecision. Leadership is associated with power that one either uses or loses. Service is rather a polite word for servitude or slavery. The servant is a "wimp." No one who aspires to the lifestyles of the rich and famous can afford to be labeled a "wimp." For the politician to be perceived as a "wimp" or weak is to invite disaster. Much time and money is spent by a candidate "looking presidential" and presenting an image to the public of "being in control." The image is crucial and the substance will take care of itself; or will it?

On closer inspection, however, we come to realize the courage and strength required for one to be a servant-leader. Robert K. Greenleaf has spent much of his life thinking about leadership. In one of his excellent pamphlets, he write, "My thesis, that more servants should emerge as leaders, or should follow only servant-leaders, is not a popular one. It is much more comfortable to go with a less demanding point of view about what is expected of one now" (*The Servant as Leader*).

The comfortable kind of leadership is the one which demands that followers follow and the leader give the orders and have the answers. The roles are clear and the expectations are never in doubt. Leaders are comfortable on their thrones and followers never have to grow up and take responsibility for their decisions and actions. Leaders receive honor and God-like obedience. Followers are rewarded with security and an "escape from freedom."

In the twenty-second chapter of Luke, Jesus gathered his disciples for a last meal. The hour had come for Jesus to drink the cup assigned by the Father. The cost of discipleship must first be paid by Jesus. Even the disciples grasped that this passover carried a message of finality about it. There was little doubt that this would be their last passover together. The forces of darkness were assembling and a showdown was inevitable. Jesus would not be long with them.

The disciples had been with Jesus for three years. They had seen the signs, heard the message, and shared the most intimate of moments with Jesus. Yet all this seemed to be for naught. A dispute broke out following the meal as to who would take over once Jesus was no longer around. Every group needs a leader. With leadership goes the power, privilege, and clout. The transcript of that last meal might read something like this:

Simon-Peter: "Let's not forget what the Master said at Caesarea Philippi."

Matthew: "Oh, yes, I remember. Jesus called you Satan and said it would be good if you advanced to the rear. I don't ever want to forget that. But I thought you would."

Simon-Peter: "A fine one you are to talk. You, a dirty tax-collector who rips off his own people for those pagan Romans."

Matthew: "It's a living and somebody has to do it. Besides, it beats fooling with all those smelly fish."

Andrew: "I think both of you smell a lot. Look, I was one of the first, if not *the* first one called by the Master. I know he looked at me first and then Simon."

Simon-Peter: "You might be my brother, but you seem to be no better than this tax-collector. You always tried to be my rival in everything."

James: "Enough of all this wimpy whining! None of you deserves to be in charge. What's needed is a strong hand at the helm."

John: "You tell 'em, brother. A few thunderbolts from
                heaven never hurt anyone. I still say that Jesus
                should have sent a message to those unbelieving
                heathens."

Judas: "All you do is talk. We need action. And money
                is where the action is. If you have enough, you
                can get what you want. Everyone has his price."

Thomas: "I have my doubts about all of you. At times, I
                am even suspicious of the Master. All that talk
                about death is so depressing. All that talk about
                resurrection is really wild. Can you imagine a
                body coming out of the grave?"

Simon-Peter: "Keep your doubts to yourself. When the time
                comes, all of us will fight for the Master. Well, *I*
                will fight for him come what may. As for the rest
                of you . . ."

The dispute was not only nasty, but it was in danger of
becoming violent. Jesus had sat and listened to it all. It was
nothing new. Humans had been saying such things for a long
time. The temptation (Jesus secretly hoped that all of this
temptation stuff had ended in the desert) was great for Jesus to
just let them tear one another apart. But he had gone this far
with them, so he might as well give it one more try.

Jesus: "You remember on the road to Caesarea Phi-
                lippi . . ."

Before he could finish, Matthew jumped in.

Matthew: "You see, Simon, I told you that you wouldn't be
                the one to lead. He's going to remind you of
                being a Satan."

Simon-Peter: "If you don't shut up, I am going to help you
                spend some of that sin money on a hospital bill."

Jesus: "What I was going to say is, on the road to
                Caesarea Philippi, I asked all of you who others
                said that I was."

Thomas:	"I remember. Yet all the answers were wrong, I think."
Jesus:	"Then I asked you, 'Who do *you* say that I am?'"
Simon-Peter:	"If you remember, I got the question right. You gave me the keys and changed my name."
Matthew:	"Don't forget, the story continues with . . ."
Simon-Peter:	"So help me, Matthew, if you dare to say it once more . . ."
Jesus:	"Enough! I have another question now. How have I shared this meal with you?"
Nathaniel:	"Kind of strange. I mean, you waited on us and you didn't even have old Martha around to cook or clean up this mess."
Philip:	"I felt uncomfortable. It was as if the roles were reversed. We should have been doing the serving."
Jesus:	"I am glad you were uncomfortable, Philip. Whenever we break the old molds and roles, there is always a feeling of strangeness. I have tried to be, with all of you, a servant-leader. All of my teachings, miracles, and confrontations were motivated by the desire to serve my Father and his Kingdom."
James:	"But, Master, you must admit that all of this seems to be a sign of weakness. You won't get many followers that way."
Jesus:	"It's not easy to be a follower of the Kingdom. You have to give up your illusions of self-control and power. The only real force is love."
Judas:	"With all due respect, Master, the only real force is money. Why, with enough money, we could get rid of the Romans and establish . . ."
Jesus:	"Establish what, Judas? We would establish nothing. All we would do is continue the forces of evil, death, and the illusion of earthly power."

Jesus soon realized that his words were having little

effect. Again, this was not unfamiliar to him. What hurt so much this time was the reality of rejection and avoidance by his intimates. Something more dramatic was required. The words needed to be made visible by action. What Jesus was saying needed to be enacted.

Philip: "What's he up to?"
Bartholomew: "How should I know? I've never quite been in the inner circle."

Jesus stood up and a hush came over the room. Would it be just more words? Was Jesus going to fashion another cord to whip them into shape? Was he simply going to walk out and leave them to their illusions? None of these. Jesus, in silence, went to each disciple and washed his feet. He performed the most menial of tasks.

Simon-Peter: "Why are you doing this? Please get up and act more like our Teacher, Lord, and yes, our Messiah."
Jesus: "You continue to want the wrong kind of Messiah. What you see as weakness is really strength. No one stands so tall as when he stoops to help those in need."
Simon-Peter: "I am sorry, but I just don't want you to do this."
Jesus: "That's your decision, Simon. But, just like I told the others at the Sea of Tiberias, you can't be with me on your terms. I told them about eating my flesh and drinking my blood, but they couldn't accept this hard teaching."
Simon-Peter: "I accepted that, didn't I? I even said you had the words of eternal life. What more do you want?"
Jesus: "I want to wash your feet. This is my hard saying for you, Simon. Listen carefully. If I don't do this, you can be in my company no longer."

Both men remained looking at each other for what seemed years. And, in a way, it was a looking back over the years. Jesus knew that if Peter was to be a true shepherd, he must learn this lesson.

Simon-Peter: "How about a bath?"

Jesus (smiling): "Can't you do anything without going to the extreme? All I want to do is wash your feet. By the way, I didn't think they were so big!"

Matthew: "Of course, his feet are so big. They have to be big, to balance that big head of his!"

Jesus: "All right, all right. I want you to see how important it is to be a servant. All of you have been called to be servants of the Kingdom. The temptations to power, money, and popularity will always be present. You will even want to lord it over one another. It is crucial that you remember what I did for you tonight. I have given you an example for all time. You who want to be leaders must keep this example alive by constantly washing feet. You who will be leaders must be found among the community as those who serve. Leaders must be the servants of the servants."

The supper continued on a more somber note. Judas left early on some business. Jesus had raised some troubling issues about betrayal and denial. Jesus got up and, with his disciples, went to the Mount of Olives. As they slowly and silently walked, Jesus wondered if they have yet understood what the passover was about. Did the words and the example have any impact? Would future generations remember the words and the example? Would those who are called to be leaders remember the One who had been among them as a servant?

2. Servant-leadership can easily become manipulative. In the name of service, we can gain control and try to become indispensable. Servant-leadership can be just as triumphalis-

tic as the autocratic parish pastor who is master of all he
surveys. The servant-leader can easily claim to know what is
best for the community. When a different plan or course of
action is proposed, the servant-leader can indulge in self-
righteous anger. Jesus was the servant-leader because he
never wanted to control anyone. Jesus' message of love was
also one of freedom. Jesus spoke the truth of the Kingdom to
the mighty, the meek, and the outcast with the hope of calling
forth the response of faith. But never did Jesus use force or
manipulation. He respected those whom he served too much.
Jesus loved the Father and desired only to do his will. Chapter
six of John's Gospel provides us with a clear example of the
servant-leader respecting the freedom of each person.

A reporter for the local paper (the *Tiberias Tabloid*)
approached Jesus.

Reporter:	"Jesus, where have you been? Everyone was looking for you after that stunt yesterday. Tell me, how did you feed so many?"
Jesus:	"If you really want a story, just tag along."
Reporter:	"What could you do to top yesterday? I mean, the crowd wanted to make you a king! You ought to think of getting a manager. I have some good contacts, you know."
Jesus:	"You mean you want to be a disciple of mine?"
Reporter:	"Sure. You call it what you want."

A crowd now gathered around Jesus, remembering what
he had done yesterday. No doubt, their full stomachs had
become empty. It was time for Jesus to do his thing.

Jesus:	"You have sought me out because I gave you something to eat. Yet here you are, hungry again. If you keep placing your hopes in a mes- siah who fills your stomach, but not your spirit, you will never be satisfied."
Benjamin (a lawyer):	"I know we don't live by bread alone, but we don't live without it."

Jesus:	"What do you mean by living? I am the one who wants to give you life eternal."
Crowd:	"How do we get this life?"
Jesus:	"You must do the will of my Father. He sent me to tell you of his unbounded love for each of you."
Reporter:	"Your father? I have it from a reliable source that your father is a carpenter."
Crowd:	"What does Joseph have to do with all this?"
Jesus:	"I am speaking about my Father in heaven. You must open your hearts and minds that God's wisdom can be yours. Take his truth in and let it become part of you."

Elam (a doctor of the law): "What is this truth? I am a man of wisdom. I have heard nothing from you. Speak plainly."

Jesus:	"You want plain speaking. Fine. Your ancestors had Moses — a great leader. My Father sent you Moses and also provided your ancestors with food in the desert. But you murmured about that just as you are doing now. Plain talk. Here goes. I am the wisdom and truth of the Father made flesh. I have come to tell you what God is about — suffering love. My Father wants to give you life eternal if only you will believe and walk in the light."

Reporter (whispering to Jesus): "Calm down, Jesus. You're losing the crowd. Regain your composure."

Jesus:	"I'll go even further. I am the bread of life. You must eat my flesh and drink my blood. If you do this, you will live. If you do not, you will perish."

A great debate erupted. Some thought that Jesus was urging them to practice cannibalism. Human sacrifice was practiced by pagans, but no self-respecting Jew would ever have considered such a thing. The crowd had been with Jesus when he had given them something to eat. Now Jesus wanted to offer them something more. He wanted to reveal the wisdom and love of God. Jesus wanted to be their communion. All of this was a hard saying.

Jesus: "You are acting as if my words are harder to believe than your full stomachs of a day ago. I am speaking to you in terms of the spirit and you continue to understand only the flesh."

Crowd: "Give us something we can hold on to. We want to believe but it is not easy. We need something visible. We need security and certainty.

Jesus: "I wonder if anything I could do would satisfy you. I have worked signs and you accused me of being a devil. I have given my words and you refused to believe."

Reporter: "I've heard enough. Too much. Jesus, you blew it. I am glad I didn't give up my job to follow you."

Slowly other followers of Jesus turned away. Some left with a deep sense of disappointment. Others had followed out of curiosity or opportunism and were soon looking for a new messiah. A dramatic moment was about to take place. Jesus now faced the Twelve.

Jesus: "Do you want to go as well?"

Judas: "Couldn't you have softened your message? The people were ready to make you their king. They were yours. The right words in the right way would have done the trick. You must be a little more prudent."

Jesus: "Judas, I came to do my Father's will. I love the people too much to spare them the truth; especially when such sparing is for my benefit. The people need to know how much the Father and I love them, and such love comes at a dear price."

James: "Never mind all that prudence and softening the message. They should never have been allowed to go away. Couldn't you have stopped them? The 'pillar of salt' approach would have been effective."

Jesus: "Effective for whom? The reality of love admits the risk of freedom. We must proclaim the truth of the Kingdom in love. In the final analysis, those who hear the word must make a decision and take responsibility for that decision."

John: "But my brother has a point. At times, the stakes are too great to allow freedom."

Jesus: "So you think freedom is a luxury that we turn on and off. You think that we can scare people into heaven. Think, John. Just what kind of God are we talking about? What kind of love is it really that takes back freedom as soon as things don't turn out the way we want? The Father loves us as human beings. Unfortunately, you want to impress with power and force. God wants to impress with the whisper of love. It is messy and it takes time. Love is patient and long-suffering. What do you think, Simon? It's unusual for you to be so quiet."

Simon-Peter: "Lord, to whom shall we go? You have the words of eternal life; and we have believed, and have come to know, that you are the Holy One of God."

It was time to move on. Jesus and the Twelve made their way to Galilee. They must avoid Judea since the authorities were ready to kill Jesus. The hour of Satan had not yet come, but it was close at hand. Even the disciples were wondering about Jesus. Some saw him as weak. Others viewed him as out of touch with reality. Many had abandoned him altogether. So many pressures, yet Jesus remained faithful to the Father. His inner strength came from knowing that the Father was with him always. Jesus gave us an example of true leadership grounded in fidelity, freedom, and love.

3. Leadership in the Christian community requires the ability to keep company with the fallen. Leadership based on power and control has little use for those who don't measure up. Muscular Christian leadership requires that we pull ourselves up by our spiritual boot straps. Leadership grounded in the need to control often seems hard on the outside. Yet such a hard exterior reveals a shallowness beneath the surface. There is little or no depth. By contrast, leadership in the image of Jesus is one that keeps company with the fallen. At first blush, this may appear to be soft. Yet on closer inspection, we come to see that the soft exterior reveals a depth of strength and commitment to the one in need. The story of Zacchaeus (Lk 19:1-10) is a case in point. A reliable eyewitness provided the following account of what happened in Jericho.

It was a normal day in Jericho. The marketplace was beginning to fill up with the sights and sounds of buying and selling. To the outsider, it seemed like chaos. To the trained eye, it was a sophisticated process of human interaction. It was about the third hour (9:00 a.m.). The Pharisees gathered on the street corner to pray so as to receive the praise of men (women were not allowed into such shallow activities). The idlers stood in the marketplace, hoping they wouldn't be hired until the eleventh hour (5:00 p.m.). Suddenly, a wave of excitement broke out. A very controversial figure was passing through.

Eleazar: "What's all the excitement? Did someone try to steal another bagel from Ben?"

David: "No. I think someone said it was that new preacher, Jesus of Nazareth."

Eleazar: "Really! I've heard a great deal about him. But so many of these guys are false. They take the denarii and run."

David: "I understand this one is different. In fact, many have even said he could be the Messiah."

Josiah (a Pharisee): "There are more Messiahs around than sand in the desert. Can you imagine the Messiah being a carpenter from nowhere? Friends of mine have said that this Jesus has no credentials."

David: "Maybe he has no diploma, but he sure knows how to draw a crowd. I haven't seen a packed house for one of your homilies."

Josiah: "Truth isn't determined by a Gamaliel poll. Ignorant people will always follow those who promise them bagels in the sky when they die."

As Jesus (for it was he) continued to move through the marketplace, the crowd continued to grow. No doubt the reports of Jesus healing the blind man near the town had added to the excitement. Jesus kept moving, though the crowd hemmed him in on all sides. Some were shouting for cures and miracles. Others were asking questions about theology. Among those in the crowd happened to be a man named Zacchaeus. He was small in stature. He was held in great contempt by the townsfolk because he was a tax collector.

Jesus (looking up in a sycamore tree): "Zacchaeus, come down before you break your neck."

Zacchaeus: "It is such an honor to meet you. I've heard a great deal about you."

Jesus: "What have you heard?"

Zacchaeus: "Oh, you know, the stories about the miracles, the way you stand up to all the self-righteous folk, and . . ."

Jesus: "And what?"

Zacchaeus: "I've heard that you're not like the other teachers. You have a special kind of authority. You look into people's hearts. You see what is good there and you remind them of it."

Jesus: "I also see what is evil in the human heart."

Zacchaeus: "Yes, but you don't throw stones. I've even

	heard that you associate with those who have a soiled identity. Is that true?"
Jesus:	"Zacchaeus, I want to come to your house. It's close to lunch time and I've had a busy morning."

Josiah (speaking to some of his disciples): "See what I told you about this Jesus. He is actually going to eat at this tax collecting sinner's house!"

Caleb (one of Josiah's disciples): "No one who truly loves God and respects the ways of our ancestors would ever have table fellowship with a sinner. This proves . . ."

Zacchaeus:	"Yes, I am a sinner. My past is not perfect or even good. But I've tried to turn around. I've made amends for my sins, to the best of my ability. I've searched out those whom I have cheated and paid them back with interest."
Jesus:	"Zacchaeus, calm down. I am glad to be a guest at your table. One day soon, I hope you'll be a guest at my table. For now, let's feed the inner man. By the way, it looks as if you could use some help around here. Do you know Lazarus' sister, Martha?"
Zacchaeus:	"Who?"
Jesus:	"Never mind."
Zacchaeus:	"Things are really different today. I mean . . . I don't know, there is just something special about having you. It's like . . ."
Jesus:	"It's like salvation, Zacchaeus. Sure, you took a wrong turn in some of your dealings with others. But the past is past. I am here to tell you that you are not just a tax collector but a son of Abraham."
Zacchaeus:	"I must admit that I don't feel I am worthy to have you in my home. I get feelings of insecurity. I know I put up a strong front but what if those outside are right?"

Jesus: "Didn't you feel a rush of joy when I called you?
What do you think made you climb that tree?
Zacchaeus, I have come to tell you of God's
unbounded love for you. Don't you know that
while we are eating there is one great party going
on right now in my Father's Kingdom? Don't give
up on yourself. My Father never will."

After lunch, Jesus rested a little, then moved on to
Jerusalem. The town of Jericho was never quite the same. The
debate continued to rage among many as to whether Jesus was
a false prophet or the Messiah. The Pharisees continued to
seek the praise of men. However, many of the people who saw,
heard, and touched Jesus felt that their lives were changed for
the better. One such man was Zacchaeus. He remained a tax
collector, but he became known as a man of fairness and
generosity. Because of Jesus, Zacchaeus never felt quite so
small again.

The Pastorals and Leadership

The ministry of Jesus is the privileged moment in the
Christian story. But the story is not frozen in time. It must
continue until he comes again in glory. The Church is entrusted with the "dangerous memory" of Jesus. The Church,
the little flock, exists in the world proclaiming Jesus as Lord.
As the Church unfolds in time, new challenges and needs
arise. As the Church approached the final third of the first
century, pastoral issues became crucial: the need for sound
teaching; establishing requirements for those who would teach
and preach; the issue of leadership; and along with sound
teaching, the need for a sound moral character by those who
lead. During times of transition (see Chapter One), these
issues become more acute. Our own time is one of transition.
We, too, face similar urgent pastoral challenges. Naturally,
each age faces its own unique challenges. However, there is
much to learn from the past.

The distant mirror of our living faith tradition begins to clear. The images begin to take shape. Three men are sitting at a table talking and sharing a meal. One of the men appears to be in his early sixties. The other two are much younger. The distant mirror is now in sharp focus. The oldest of the three is the Apostle Paul and his partners in conversation are Timothy and Titus. We are also able to hear some of their exchanges.

Paul:	"Well, tell me, Titus, how are things going in Crete?"
Titus:	"All right, I guess. But's it's so hard to find a few good men. I'd even settle for a Lydia."
Paul:	"I know what you mean. Many a time my so-called partners in the Gospel got going when the going got tough. I've done my best to forgive Mark. What seems to be the major obstacle?"
Titus:	"The circumcision party has been very effective. A lot of the old guard hankers after the good old days. It's Moses this and Moses that. They promise the people certainty and security. And, of course, they appeal to their pride as God's exclusive people. This is hard to resist in these times."
Timothy:	"I know what you mean, Titus. Things haven't been going all that well at Ephesus. I have to contend with those who appeal to the people by telling stories which tickle ears. The teachers tell the people what they think they want to hear. Some even proclaim a strict obedience to the Law which leaves no room for grace. I guess it gives one a sense of superiority or self-righteousness."
Paul:	"All you are saying is not unfamiliar to me. Throughout my many travels, I've had to contend with false teachers and flashy doctrines. I'll never forget those foolish Galatians. The temptation is always present to turn around and seek comfort in a secure, if illusionary, past."
Titus:	"How did you handle the situation?"

Paul: "There's no easy answer. There's no blueprint or magic technique for controlling people. I know. I've tried my share of controlling. The results were disastrous. I've had some interesting times at Corinth."

Timothy: "At times, I wonder if I am being effective. I have some serious doubts."

Titus: "Me, too. You've put me in charge and I feel like a failure. I have to admit that some of those other preachers are more exciting. Some of their teachings really attract the students. What am I doing wrong?"

Paul: "Get over your self-pity. Remember you are called to be faithful. The Lord will judge the rest. Look, I can remember how it was when I first started out. I wanted to save the world. However, someone did the job before me."

Titus and Timothy were stone-faced at even this little attempt by Paul to be humorous. Religion and smiling didn't go together. Or so they thought.

Paul: "Boys, brighten up a little. It's amazing what a smile can do. Anyway, when I started out, I was going to be effective and popular. I tried to preach Jesus in terms of Greek philosophy. Needless to say, the results were anything but stunning. Some even mocked me. Later on, I decided that if I was going to be mocked, it would be for the Gospel and not for trying to please all the people all the time."

Timothy: "It's more than the message. The messenger needs to be faithful as well. Too often, there is correct doctrine, but it is not put into practice."

Paul: "No doubt about it. Without a sound moral character, our teaching, if I may quote myself from another context, is just words, "a noisy gong and a clanging cymbal.""

Timothy: "Another thing, Paul. I am so young. All this seems beyond my resources."

Paul: "That's a great insight. Ministry is beyond your resources, if all you have is *your* resources. If that's the case, then your work is one big ego-trip. Let me lay it out for you and Titus: You will have to risk being unpopular. At times, you will have to preach the hard truth rather than the comfortable compromise. Some will leave. That is their decision. All we can do is commend them to the Lord's grace and care."

Titus: "Since we're laying things out, Paul, let me say this. If we have done such a good job of leading people, why do we have all this controversy?"

Paul: "Not all controversy and questioning are bad, Titus. When people care deeply and feel great commitments, they are going to voice their opinions. For all of my struggles with the Corinthians, I sure did enjoy the contest. I was forced to think and reexamine all my too comfortable beliefs. I had become complacent about my teachings on marriage, resurrection, and the Lord's Supper. They shook me up. And I needed that."

Timothy: "You can't mean that all the trouble Titus and I are experiencing is a good thing."

Paul: " Learn to distinguish, Timothy. That will come with age. Sorry, I didn't mean to bring up the age thing. Maybe one day, people will honor youth. Anyway, there is a good conscience disagreement and then there is the disagreement which comes from bad faith. I mean the person who challenges the accepted teaching out of selfish concerns. Such a person loves controversy for its own sake. This kind of teacher wants the status of celebrity. From what I know, Timothy, you and Titus are dealing with bad faith teachers and preachers."

Titus:	"I have a tough day tomorrow. I have to face the Cretans. That's not an easy task. What am I going to do?"
Paul:	"Simple. Tell them the truth. But do it with love. And please invite others to help. There are good people there. Appeal to their finer sides. Don't let the wicked triumph by blinding you to the goodness and grace which abound."
Timothy:	"What about me?"
Paul:	"Yes, Timothy, what about you indeed. The challenge is for you to remain strong. I don't mean a macho or romantic view of ministry. At this point, your greatest need is internal. Cooperate with the Spirit which dwells in you. In your weakness, let Christ be your strength. Keep yourself pure and avoid all scandal. Finally, be open to the grace which will sustain you in times of loneliness and persecution. Let those entrusted to you draw strength from the grace shining through your limitations."
Titus:	"I always feel renewed after our talks. I have so many more questions."
Paul:	"It's getting late. We all have a full day tomorrow. We will get together again on other matters. For now, we need some sleep. Grace and peace be with you both."

The three men separated and returned to their homes. Yet much abided. The bond between them could not be broken by distance or age. Tomorrow they would face their own challenges. But they would draw strength from the one same Spirit and from the grace they have been to each other.

A Philosophical Note: A.N. Whitehead, God, and Leadership

Catholic theology has understood itself as "faith seeking understanding." The "Catholic thing," when it comes to theology, is one of befriending reason and philosophy. We are to love the Lord with our "whole mind." We believe that there is an indispensable contribution made by reason for knowing and loving God. The "mind's road to God" is an exciting adventure. St. Augustine turned to Plato and St. Thomas to Aristotle so as to better explain those truths ever old and ever new. Revelation and reason are not enemies. Human reason is a gift from God which is elevated by the grace of revelation to true wisdom. Augustine and Aquinas could turn to the philosophers because they believed all truth to be one, and that the oneness of truth led to the One True God.

Catholic theology in the contemporary world once again seeks to explain the truths of the faith in a way that is intelligible and faithful. We no longer live in the intellectual and cultural worlds of Augustine and Aquinas. We live in the closing decades of the twentieth century. Our challenge, however, is to do what they did. Namely, we are to find creative and intelligent ways of communicating the faith. We are to draw on these rich resources of our tradition as well as the new insights of our own historical moment. We must be wise enough to preserve the past and confident enough in the Spirit to be open to new discoveries. In doing so, we shall be like the "householder who brings out of his treasures what is new and what is old" (Mt 13:52).

The philosophical writings of Alfred North Whitehead have helped provide such a (but by no means the only) creative new approach to Christian theology. Catholic theologians have not been unaffected by his writings. In fact, Catholic theology, with its strong tradition of befriending philosophy, has benefited from Whiteheadian categories. The dynamic, process view of reality which is at the center of Whitehead's thought is congruent with our understanding of the Church as the pilgrim people of God, journeying to the New Jerusalem. Bernard Lee, in his excellent book, *The Becoming of the Church*, writes: "Instead of understanding the Church as a place or thing or substantively understood society, it is seen to be an event whose process is reality." The Church is the historical, concrete unfolding of the mystery of God's love in time on the way to that time beyond time. The abiding presence of the Spirit continues to call the people of God to greater intensities of love, community, joy, and peace.

Whitehead's concept of God and the event of Jesus offers us some valuable insights concerning pastoral leadership. For Whitehead, God possesses a tripolar nature: primordial, consequent, and subjective.

The primordial nature is "God alone with himself." This aspect of the nature of God is the pure possibility of all reality. All of the eternal objects or forms are contained here. The primordial nature of God is the wholly other and unknowable aspect of God. The primordial nature is the divine mystery, which no human can know or penetrate. Before an entity becomes actual, it is in the primordial nature of God as pure potential. The primordial nature of God contains his purpose or aim for each entity as well as the aim or hope for all creation. The primordial nature of God stands above time. This is the transcendence of God, the Ancient One who remains in the beyond.

God is not only transcendent. He is also immanent. God is in a real relationship with the world. The consequent nature of God is all of physical reality, every entity, no matter how great or small, taken into himself and felt by God. From the smallest movement in the most distant galaxy to the cosmic explosions of new worlds, all are felt by God. It is important to say that Whitehead is not advocating pantheism. God is not the world. Rather, we may understand God's consequent relationship with the world as "panpantheism" (see John Cobb's excellent book, *God and the World*), that is, God is affected or moved by the world and the world is moved by God. What goes on in the world really matters to God. God has a real interest in the becoming of the world as more intense, harmonious, and beautiful.

God does not simply create all that is and provide it with its initial aim or purpose. He also cares for each entity and its becoming to be what it is. Furthermore, God cares beyond the perishing of each entity. God's care overcomes the power of death. The subjective nature of God (this aspect of God is very much debated by Whiteheadian scholars, for some hold that it is not a distinct nature but a part of the consequent nature) preserves all that is good and noble by taking it into God. In effect, God saves and cherishes everything of value and offers it back to the world. The past lives in the present and helps to form the future. God's love is faithful and everlasting. For example, the acts of love or generosity we perform do not stop or perish with a particular episode. Rather, these acts or events are taken up into God and offered back to the world to encourage greater and more intense love and generosity. Even the evil that is done is taken up into God and transformed by his all-powerful love. Whatever good there is, however small or invisible to us, is experienced by God. The power of God is his ability to confront evil and transform it by love. The horror of war or the brokenness of a marriage are taken into God. God continually offers these back to us in the hope that we will learn to find more constructive and harmonious ways to settle our conflicts. We often learn slowly. Our God is patient and his love endures forever.

This beautiful and complex nature of God, especially God's relation to the world, raises an important question: How does God relate to the world? In scholastic philosophy, we would ask: What is God's agency toward the world? In more modern terms, we would ask: What is God's style of interacting with the world? This is no trivial question, for by understanding how God relates to the world, we can come to understand how we are expected to relate to one another. The leader of the community of faith would be the one who would relate in an agency or style similar to that by which God relates to the world.

From the moment each entity (human person, plant, cloud, etc.) comes into existence, God provides the entity with its initial aim. This initial aim is God's plan or hope for that entity in terms of its own becoming and that of the world as a whole. God knows what is best and, from the beginning, God aims each entity towards its fulfillment. However, we are free and we need not respond to this aim or hope. We can do our own thing apart from God. We can assert our will (subjective aim) apart from the whole. Yet God will not cancel the initial aim or destroy the freedom. Rather, God struggles with the person and continually offers him new opportunities to reform. In effect, God cares for us and wants what is best for us individually and in terms of the community. However, God does not cancel our freedom in order to obtain a quick resolution. God labors with us and the whole of creation.

Some of the most beautiful passages in Whitehead concern God's relationship with the world. Whitehead makes it clear that God is not a dictator or a Caesar. God uses a minimum amount of control and a maximum amount of love. God does not want to control and dominate us. God relates to the world through persuasion. Consider these passages from Whitehead, which could easily serve for spiritual reading:

> When the Western world accepted Christianity, Caesar conquered; and the received text of Western theology was edited by his lawyers. The Code of Justinian is two volumes expressing one movement of the human spirit. The brief Galilean vision of humility flickered throughout the ages, uncertainly. In the official formulation of religion . . . the deeper idolatry, of the fashioning of God in the image of the Egyptian, Persian, and Roman imperial rulers, was retained. The Church gave unto God the attributes which belonged exclusively to Caesar.

> The revolts of destructive evil, purely self-regarding, are dismissed into their triviality of merely individual facts; and yet the good they did achieve in individual joy, in individual sorrow, in the introduction of needed contrast, is yet saved by its relation to the complete whole. The image — and it is but an image — the image under which this operative growth of God's nature is best conceived, is that of a tender care that nothing be lost.
> The consequent nature of God is his judgment on the

world. He saves the world as it passes into the immediacy of his own life. It is the judgment of a tenderness which loses nothing that can be saved. It is also the judgment of a wisdom which uses what in the temporal world is mere wreckage.

Another image which is also required to understand his consequent nature, is that of his infinite patience . . . we conceive of the patience of God, tenderly saving the turmoil of the intermediate world by the completion of his own nature.

God's role is not the combat of productive force with productive force, of destructive force with destructive force; it lies in the patient operation of the overpowering rationality of his conceptual harmonization. He does not create the world, he saves it; or, more accurately, he is the poet of the world, with tender patience leading it by his vision of truth, beauty, and goodness. (*Process and Reality: An Essay in Cosmology*, pp. 519-533.)

Alfred North Whitehead, in 1933, published a book entitled *Adventures of Ideas*. In this work, Whitehead drew on the insights of modern science to formulate the following principle: "A thing is what it does." We come to know things by what they do; for in doing, there is revelation. God, too, gives us a revelation of himself in his doing: creating, liberating, challenging, and reconciling. But above all, what God does is save. The Hebrew Bible speaks of God's saving activity. A most significant moment was the Exodus experience.

In the fullness of time, God's very saving activity would become visible in the person of Jesus. In Jesus, the unity of God and humanity reach perfection. Jesus is the God-man who reveals the nature of God as suffering, patient love. Jesus reveals what it means to be truly human: a oneness of aims in which the will of the Father is perfectly followed in loving obedience. The uniqueness of Jesus is that the presence of God was so complete in him, so enfleshed in him, that the disciples experienced Jesus as the Christ of God. Reflecting on this experience, the Church is able to say throughout the ages:

Jesus is true God of true God; begotten not made, one in being with the Father; and Jesus is Lord. The Church also confesses Jesus to be true man of true man. Process theologian Norman Pittenger has written the following about the uniqueness of Jesus as well as his similarity to us:

> Jesus Christ includes, not excludes, all that is truly human; he defines, but he does not confine, the ceaseless working of God "for us men and for our salvation." If he were entirely different, he would be entirely meaningless to us. Because he is "one of us," yet distinctively himself in what he was called to accomplish, he can be both our Brother and our Lord and Savior. It is his being "one with us" that makes it possible for him to bring us newness of life or redemption; it is because he is distinctively himself that it is truly possible for him to do just this . . . in Christ he makes it clear, in a vivid, compelling, signal, and effectual fashion what he — the cosmic Lover or God — *is always doing* for his children. And hence he enables us to make a response of equal intensity. (*Catholic Faith in a Process Perspective*)

The event of Jesus (what Whitehead calls "the brief Galilean vision") makes visible the nature of God as patient, suffering love. Jesus did not use manipulation or coercion to achieve his aims. Jesus came among us as one who invited all men and women of good will to respond to God's love and presence. Jesus appealed to the better moments and aspects of the human condition. He spoke with the authority of love rather than the force of fear. Again and again he went in search of the lost, the alienated, the sinner, and the outcast. Jesus' whole life and death serve as a constant reminder and challenge to the principalities and powers that only love lasts and achieves the final victory. In table fellowship with the uncelebrated, in being poor among the poor, and by living among us as one who served, Jesus left us an example of how we are to be with one another. The life and death of Jesus, understood by the world as defeat, is the supreme victory. On the cross, the ultimate revelation of God's nature occurred: God is SUFFERING LOVE. It is only such a love which can defeat sin and death. Only such love and hope and faith can proclaim, "he is not to be found among the dead for he is risen. He lives!"

The agency of God with the world and the event of Jesus contain crucial implications for Church ministry and leadership. The Church is that event in history which keeps alive the "dangerous memory" of Jesus. The danger of this memory cannot be minimized. It challenges the earthly kingdoms to recognize the truth of God's sovereignty. Lasting power does not come from the chariot, the ICBM, or a rising Gross National Product. True security is never gained by trusting absolutely in the work of all too human hands. The response of the world is the same now as it was when he walked among us: ridicule, apathy, labels that libel, and, finally, violence and death.

The memory of Jesus is dangerous for the Church. It reminds us that we are to love one another as he loved. The cost of discipleship entails carrying our cross daily and facing Jerusalem. From those to whom much is given, much is expected in terms of humble service. The real authority for preaching and teaching resides in fidelity to the person of Jesus. And this person of Jesus reveals to us the ways to eternal life: to love God with one's whole being; to be for others as much as we are for ourselves; to search for the lost and celebrate those who return to their Father's house; to proclaim the words of forgiveness and acceptance with a kiss of peace and the oil of gladness; to lay aside the trappings and illusions of force and put on the breastplate of patient, suffering love; and, in the midst of a world which passes away, proclaim that new creation when he will be all in all. The force of the Church is the force of love which endures so many defeats on the way to that final victory won by the Man of Sorrows. The enduring power of the Church is to abide in the world through the power of the Spirit. And the authority of those who lead comes from serving in imitation of the One who was in our midst as Servant of the servants.

III

TO TEACH WITH AUTHORITY

Among the most important of pastoral ministries carried on by the Church, the pastoral ministry of teaching ranks at or near the top. Unfortunately, perhaps because of the contemporary lack of esteem for teachers or the conflict within the Church over various teachings, this ministry has fallen on hard times. Yet we must keep in mind that Jesus calls himself a "teacher" and sends off the disciples to teach all the nations the good news of salvation. The Church of Jesus Christ is a teaching Church. Archbishop Rembert G. Weakland, O.S.B. has written the following about the teaching mission of the Church:

> If teaching was listed first among the tasks of Jesus in his mission, should it not be one of our primary concerns also as Church? There is a tendency among us to reduce our religion to just the healing, the physical concerns (note so many TV electronic-church programs), or just proclaiming the good news, as if that in itself is sufficient and the Spirit will take over. Jesus put teaching first. He knew that his message would require a new way of acting, a new way of responding to God and neighbor. He knew that his life and ministry had to be seen in the light of the history of God's people that went before. (*All God's People*)

The Catholic approach to the doing of theology requires sound teaching and dedicated teachers. We Catholics hold that theology is "faith seeking understanding." We are of the belief that faith and reason work together in a covenant which brings the community to know, love, and serve God. The Catholic tradition is one which befriends intelligence and believes that "grace favors the well-prepared mind." We have no fear of what science may uncover and the social sciences tell us about the human person. We are comfortable in the presence of all truth since all truth leads to the God who is its author and perfection. The latest discoveries and deepest insights are cause for rejoicing. They further reveal the mystery of God's love, beauty, and intelligence. The teaching vocation is just that, a vocation, a call from God to proclaim his wonder throughout the earth. The Second Vatican Council, in its document on Christian education, affirms the dignity of the Christian teacher and the awesome responsibility assumed by such teachers:

> This sacred Synod urgently implores young people themselves to be aware of the excellence of the teaching vocation, and to be ready to undertake it with a generous spirit, especially in those parts of the globe where a shortage of teachers is causing a crisis in the training of the young. This same Synod . . . entreats them (teachers) to carry on magnanimously in their chosen task and to strive to excel in penetrating their students with the spirit of Christ, in the art of teaching, and in the advancement of knowledge. Thus, they will not only foster the internal renewal of the Church, but will safeguard and intensify her beneficial presence in the world of today, especially the world of the intellect. (*Declaration on Christian Education*)

These powerful words of the Council Fathers were not meant to remain on paper, but to be put into practice in dioceses throughout the world. In November of 1972, the National Conference of Catholic Bishops (NCCB) published a pastoral message on Catholic education entitled *To Teach as Jesus Did*. The document contains a recognition and a deep appreciation of the teaching ministry as essential to the life of the Church. This ministry is not a luxury or one to be exercised at a later and more convenient hour. The teaching ministry is entrusted to the Church by Jesus. And now is the acceptable time and urgent hour for the teaching ministry. The history of humankind is at a crossroads. Some are prophets of gloom and doom. Others raise their voices in naive optimism, grounded in our technical power. The world asks of the Church: Is there any word from the Lord? The Church has been given a graced moment of ministry. A great twentieth century prophet and convert to Catholicism, Malcolm Muggeridge, has written the following:

> . . . rejoice that we see around us at every hand the decay of the institutions and instruments of power, see intimations of empires falling to pieces, money in total disarray, dictators and parliamentarians alike nonplussed by the confusion and conflicts which encompass them. For it is precisely when every earthly hope has been explored and found wanting, when every possibility of help from earthly sources has been sought and is not forthcoming, when every recourse this world offers, moral as well as material, has been explored to no effect, when in the shivering cold the last faggot has been thrown on the fire and in the gathering darkness every glimmer of light has finally flickered out, it's then that Christ's hand reaches out, sure and firm. Then Christ's words bring their inexpressible comfort, then His light shines brightest, abolishing the darkness forever. So finding in everything only deception and nothingness, the soul is constrained to have recourse to God Himself and to rest content with him. (*The End of Christendom*)

In this hour of history, *our* hour and we have no other, so many of the idols of the Enlightenment and the contemporary world are found wanting: intelligence without wisdom; power without moral purpose; freedom without direction; and human reason without a transcendent goal. The good news of salvation must be taught, preached, and lived to the whole world. The message of the Kingdom of God is not a private affair of the heart, but a message which renews the face of the earth. Simply put, we teach the good news as a people of Pentecost, a new Pentecost. The noted Jesuit teacher and evangelist, Father Johannes Hofinger, S.J. once wrote:

> What we need more than anything else in the present situation is a new Pentecost, a new and deep religious experience of the basic elements of faith and life. It can only be obtained in prayer, but it can renew all sectors of Christian activity. We humbly expect it as an undeserved gift from God's mercy, for we know he will give it if we approach him humbly in prayer and open ourselves to his grace. This gift of a loving Father begins with a thorough conversion in the spirit of true and therefore living repentance. It cannot be obtained by manipulation, by mere human planning or skillful organization. (*Evangelization & Catechesis*)

Father Hofinger, in another work on the pastoral ministry of teaching, lent his powerful voice and keen insights to the urgent need for a timely catechesis in the Spirit: "If catechesis in the power of the Spirit is the only authentic catechesis, it is, of course, always timely but there is something about our times which lends a particular urgency to the task of attending to the charismatic dimensions of our work" (*Pastoral Life in the Power of the Spirit*). The Church entrusted with the pastoral ministry of teaching must teach as Jesus did. It is to the Teacher that we now turn our attention.

To Teach as Jesus Did

How did Jesus teach? The simple answer is provided by Matthew's Gospel at the end of the Sermon on the Mount: "And when Jesus finished these sayings, the crowds were astonished at his teachings, for he taught them as one who had authority, and not as their scribes" (Mt 7:28). The teaching of the scribes was a repetition of the tradition handed on from the past. The scribes offered teachings they had received from other scribes and rabbis. Unlike the scribes, and even the prophets, Jesus taught with the authority of his own word and person. Jesus did not say, "Thus says the Lord," but rather, "You have heard it was said . . . But I say to you . . ." Jesus is one who teaches a new law which perfects the old one. Jesus offers a new covenant which completes the Sinai covenant. Jesus challenges all who wish to follow him to live in a new way — the way of the Spirit which alone gives life. The Jesus who teaches with authority does not reject the past or tradition as much as he perfects and completes it. "Think not that I have come to abolish the law and the prophets; I have come not to abolish them but to fulfil them" (Mt 5:17). To teach the law and the prophets is to teach about Jesus.

The Gospels contain a number of instances in which Jesus is active in the teaching ministry. In the following three episodes, we are presented with important aspects of the teaching ministry. These three "teachable moments" in the life of Jesus speak to us about the following: effective teaching invites the disciple to move from the physical to the spiritual, from the seen to the unseen; and, finally, effective teaching must often face opposition. Thus, the effective teacher finds himself often in need of grace so as to remain faithful to the mission.

The reputation of Jesus as a teacher was spreading throughout the district of Capernaum and the surrounding region. The opposition was growing as well. This son of a carpenter was able to move the minds and hearts of the people with his message and manner. Jesus was a teacher with authority. Yet the message was one of liberation and joy. The good news teaching of Jesus was a burden only to those who were convinced of their own righteousness and the truth of their teaching. By contrast, Jesus spoke to those who were ignored, forgotten, rejected, and assigned to the rear of the temple. Jesus taught in such a way that he challenged his audience to think, value, and live in a new way. The old categories and world views were no longer adequate. God was doing a new thing. Jesus was in their midst teaching that fear could be replaced by love. The old barriers were being replaced with the bridges of reconciliation.

Eliphaz (a leading lawyer): "Jesus, it is an honor to have you with our discussion group. Your reputation is well known to us. I, for one, admire the self-educated teacher. Naturally, though, not everyone is as open-minded as I am."

Jesus: "I am happy to be with you. As you know, I accept invitations from all kinds of people. Just last week, I had lunch with Zacchaeus. Some of your friends were upset. I guess they are not as open-minded as you about lunch as well!"

Eliphaz: "Well, enough about that. Let's get down to cases. As a great teacher, tell us what is required to inherit eternal life."

Jesus: "As a 'great teacher,' let me clarify the question. Eternal life is not something we inherit. It is not a legal issue, but a pure gift from our loving God. What is required is the ability to accept gifts in a gracious way."

Eliphaz: "What do you mean by a 'gracious way'?"

Jesus: "I mean that we must learn how to love and be generous with the gifts we have been given. Too often, gifts become possessions. They are used to build up our self-esteem at the expense of others. Isn't that really what the law is about — love of God?"

Eliphaz: "Well, yes. We are to love God with our whole being."

Jesus: "And what else?"

Eliphaz: "We are to love our neighbor as ourselves."

Jesus: "That's the tough part, isn't it? To love ourselves and our neighbor. We are often kept from ac-

cepting God's love and sharing that love because
we don't feel we are worthy of God's love. Our
sin is too much before us. We won't allow the sin
to give way to grace and healing. Yet only when
amazing grace lifts the veil of sin do we see one
another as members of the one family of our
loving Father. To so love and be loved is to know
what eternal life is all about."

The discussion group comprised of these learned and
wise men grew silent. Such a teacher and teaching had never
been among them before. The eyes of all were fixed on Jesus.
Finally, many in the group began to praise Jesus for his
insights. However, Eliphaz grew resentful of the attention paid
to Jesus. He thought that this mere carpenter's son had up-
staged him. Eliphaz was not about to let Jesus add this session
to his *vitae* of successes. Eliphaz was armed with another
question.

Eliphaz: "You have spoken well, Teacher. But you raise
an interesting issue which is much debated by
scholars and lawyers. Namely, just who is my
neighbor? After all, we need to know clearly and
precisely to whom we owe this debt of love. If
you can help clarify the debate, we will be most
grateful and you will indeed be a great teacher."

Jesus: "I guess one of the perils of being a lawyer is that
you always think like a lawyer. Everything with
you, Eliphaz, is a legal issue or a discussion of
the facts. Truth is deeper than facts. Life doesn't
fit our neat categories. We can't treat people as
if they are nothing but legal issues to be decided. Eliphaz, don't you see that 'neighbor' is
not a concept, but a living reality. 'Neighbor' is a
word that connects with flesh and blood."

Eliphaz: "You have to have limits. You seem to be calling
us to a kind of chaos. Do you really think that we

can live in a world in which everyone is my neighbor? That's not, excuse me, very realistic. Jesus, you need to be more specific."

Jesus: "You make a good point, Eliphaz. There is a danger in saying that everyone is your neighbor. In truth, this can be an escape. There are many people who love humanity but not the individual human beings with whom they daily interact. What are you suggesting?"

Eliphaz: "The traditional categories have worked well. Why fix what isn't broken? The neighbor is a fellow Jew, a lawyer, or member of the family, and, within limits, those who live in the same district."

Jesus: "What about those who don't fit any of these categories? Who takes care of them? Who shows them love?"

Eliphaz: "We can't save the whole world. We're human, you know. There is only so much we can do. Could you imagine including some — Well, you know what I mean. Let me ask you, Jesus, what are you suggesting?"

Jesus: "Let me tell you a story. A man was going down to Jericho, and he fell among many robbers, who stripped him and beat him, and departed, leaving him half dead. Now, by chance, a priest was going down the road; and when he saw him, he passed on the other side. So, likewise a Levite, when he came to the place and saw him, passed by on the other side. But a Samaritan, as he journeyed, came to where he was; and when he saw him, he had compassion, and went to him and bound up his wounds, pouring on oil and wine; then he set him on his own beast and brought him to an inn, and took care of him. And the next day he took out two denarii and gave them to the innkeeper saying, 'Take care of him;

and whatever more you spend, I will repay you when I come back.' Which of these three, do you think, proved neighbor to the man who fell among the robbers?"

Eliphaz: "The one who showed mercy to him."

Jesus: "You mean the Samaritan. Can't you even say the word?"

Eliphaz: "Yes. The Samaritan. But this is just a story. I know that life isn't that way. Why, right now, I bet a Samaritan is up to no good on the road to Jericho. I bet the guy who was mugged fell victim to a Samaritan!"

Jesus: "Your cynicism, Eliphaz, is really fear. You are so afraid of thinking and acting in a new way. You have too much invested in old hatreds and past certainties. Yet it is only if you let go of these that you will experience peace and joy. Stories of God are dangerous because they invite you to tell your personal story with him as the main character. I hope you will take the risk and even be willing to learn from this Samaritan."

Slowly the weekly meeting of Eliphaz's discussion group broke up. Many wanted to know if Jesus would come back. Others found his teachings both unsophisticated and offensive. No one was left without an opinion about this Teacher. At a subsequent meeting of the group, some participants were passing the word that Eliphaz has been seen speaking with "a known Samaritan." Some members of the group were in a real panic, for there was a rumor that Eliphaz was going to invite a Samaritan to attend the next meeting. What next — Tax collectors? Women? Even some sinners? Some members were beginning to see just how dangerous these stories of Jesus could be.

One of those who attended the weekly discussions in Eliphaz's house was a very influential and devout man named Nicodemus. He was a Pharisee and a member of the ruling

body known as the Sanhedrin. Nicodemus couldn't get Jesus
and his stories out of his mind. Being a man of integrity, he
wanted to know more about this Teacher and his wisdom.
However, some members of the Sanhedrin were suspicious of
Nicodemus. They accused him of being too liberal and being in
sympathy with Jesus. Yet Nicodemus felt a profound need to
meet with Jesus again. So, under the cover of night, he went in
search of Jesus to find out where he stayed.

Nicodemus (knocking on Jesus' door): "I am Nicodemus. I once
heard you teach at one of Eliphaz's weekly discussions. I need to speak with you. May I come
in?"

Jesus (opening the door and smiling): "Nicodemus, please
come in. It is usually I who am knocking on
doors and asking to come in. It's a nice switch."

Nicodemus: "After your teaching, I and others came to the
conclusion that you are a man of God. Your
words and deeds are like no other teacher we
have known. I want to know more of your truth."

Jesus: "God's truth is for all who believe in him and the
one he has sent. Yet this truth does not come
from works, moral worth, or personal achievements. Nicodemus, you must be born again."

Nicodemus: "You can't be serious. No one goes back into his
mother's womb."

Jesus: "I am not speaking about a physical rebirth.
Naturally, you cannot return to the womb. How-
ever, supernaturally you must be born anew as a
child of God. Such a rebirth is the work of the
Spirit. The Spirit cannot be confined or restricted by dogmas and ceremonies. The Spirit
is sent by me and the Father."

Nicodemus: "Even though I have spent my life studying the
traditions, I do not understand what you are
saying."

Jesus: "Why not? You are a great teacher of the law.

Yet how difficult it is for you and the learned to understand the wisdom of God. You saw how Eliphaz and his friends refused to believe. They love their comfortable teachings. They like to use religion for their own power."

Nicodemus: "Aren't you asking too much? You speak about such mysterious and deep things. We simply can't understand."

Jesus: "Can't or won't? You will never understand the things of God if you rely on your own wisdom and abilities. But you don't have to. God has sent the Son of Man to keep you in the truth. What you find hard is the need to be transformed by the Spirit who alone gives life. What you find troubling is the need to look beyond the physical in order to see the Supreme Spiritual reality!"

Nicodemus: "Jesus, tell me what this Supreme Spiritual reality is!"

Jesus: "This reality is in front of you and working within you. The Supreme Spiritual reality is God's faithful, suffering love. God so loved you and his creation that he sent the Son so that all who believe will have eternal life. God is not about condemnation and rejection. God desires everyone to know him and experience his love and peace."

Nicodemus: "What about those who don't believe?"

Jesus: "Again, I must say to you that God did not send the Son to condemn. Condemnation comes from those who refuse to believe. God respects human freedom. The Son is simply a light which brings to light the deeds and motives of human beings. Those in sin flee the light. Those who love God seek the light of his truth."

Nicodemus: "Deep in my heart, I know you are a teacher from God, by the way in which you speak. I want to walk in the light."

Jesus:　　　　"And so you will. I know you have taken a big risk coming to see me. Don't judge the final outcome by what happens now. Immediate results are often deceiving. The Father is patient. You need to be patient as well. Sometimes it is hard for teachers to be patient with students. It is even harder to be patient with yourself."

Nicodemus:　　"Jesus, I am not sure what the future holds. I don't know if we will meet again. Yet I do know that I am not the same man since I met you."

Nicodemus left the place where Jesus was staying. The night was giving way to the dawn. The first rays of the sun were making their appearance over the crest of the hills and the floor of the desert.

As the years went by, Nicodemus continued the process of rebirth in the Spirit. He was seen less and less in the company of Eliphaz and the weekly discussion group. The Sanhedrin wrote him off as a lost cause. Nicodemus was no longer on the inside of decision-making. Finally, the break came. As the hour of God's supreme revelation in Jesus on the Cross is completed, we have the following true testimony:

> After this Joseph of Arimathea, who was a disciple of Jesus, but secretly, for fear of the Jews, asked Pilate that he might take away the body of Jesus, and Pilate gave him leave. So he came and took the body. Nicodemus also, who had at first come to him by night, came bringing a mixture of myrrh and aloes, about a hundred pounds' weight. They took the body of Jesus, and bound it in linen cloths with the spices, as is the burial custom of the Jews. (Jn 19:38-40)

Nicodemus, the teacher who had come by night, was now a born again child of the light. The man who had risked so much was present at the moment when the forces of evil were enjoying their greatest victory. Yet Nicodemus, a teacher, had learned the great lesson from the Teacher. Nicodemus knew that the end was really the beginning and that death would give way to eternal life.

The great American philosopher and educator, John Dewey, once wrote that education is not preparation for life, but life itself. Every teacher is entrusted with preparing minds and hearts for the future. There comes a time when the teacher must let go and allow the disciple to face life on his or her own. There is a classroom beyond the classroom. Life educates as well as the lecture and the textbook. The teacher must stand back and allow the disciples to face the challenge of putting theory into practice. The teacher is filled with anxiety. Have I taught enough? Too much? Will they be able to confront the challenges without me? Will the disciples forget me? Have I taught them to be mature with their freedom and responsible with their knowledge? All of these questions and countless others swirl in the mind of the teacher.

No doubt the same feelings of anxiety and pride were in the heart of Jesus as he sent the twelve disciples on their first mission. To date, they had heard the preaching, witnessed the miracles, and been privileged to be schooled in the intimate teachings of the Kingdom. It was now time for them to be sent into the world. Jesus called them together for some final instructions.

Jesus: "It is now time for you to take an active part in the work of the Kingdom. You will teach, preach, and heal. I hope you have learned the lessons I have shared with you since the beginning."

James: "I can't wait to face those Gentiles, especially the Samaritans. Wait until they hear what I have to say. They will be converted or else!"

Jesus: "I want you and your brother, John, in fact, I want all of you, to avoid those places and people. Others will come later to care for the Gentiles. For now, you are to go among your own people and proclaim the Kingdom."

Thomas: "I hope I am ready for such work. I have my doubts. Remember, Jesus, I was absent for some of your teachings. Philip's notes weren't too clear or complete."

Simon-Peter: "Don't any of you worry about a thing. I have everything planned. Look at all the provisions I brought along. We won't want for a thing."

Jesus: "Leave all of those things here. Gold, silver, food, and clothes are not going to sustain you. You must rely on God's loving care and the generosity of those whom you serve. You will be living on the boundary. You will need to find those in the town who are leaders and work with them. Enlist their support. In other words, don't think that you know it all or that you have to do it all."

Andrew: "I must confess that I am nervous. I am not sure I can measure up to what is expected of me. I might fail."

Jesus: "Of course you will fail, Andrew. We all do. But that doesn't mean you're a failure. You will need to learn to live with human rejection. You will be challenging people to live a new way. You will be asking them to do what is most painful — change. Remember how it was when you and Simon had to leave your homes to follow me. Hostility is often the result of fear. The only thing which overcomes fear is love. Love will transform *your* fear into confidence. Love will transform *their* fear into an openness to the message of the Kingdom."

Andrew: "But I am not you. You are a success. Even some of the Pharisees have followed you. You teach with authority."

Jesus: "Andrew, how selective is your memory! Don't you also remember the Pharisees calling me Beelzebub? Need I remind you of the time in the synagogue in Capernaum when they wanted to end my career just as it was starting? Let's face it, my name is not associated with peace and quiet. I've never lied to you. I want you and the others to know this: if they have called me all manner of vile names, how much more will they speak ill of you."

Judas: "It's not so much the words that bother me. I am afraid of the physical abuse we will have to take. Also, I am told that the authorities might arrest us. What are we to do then?"

Jesus: "Two responses, Judas. First of all, there will be opposition and it will come from those within your own family. There are few pains to match betrayal within a family. Persecutions are to be expected as well. The temptation will be great to deny me. But remember, and this is the second thing, Judas, remember that you never do the work of the Kingdom alone. The Father's loving, courageous protection is always with you. The Father loves each of you so much that the strands of your hair are counted. You will never be abandoned. You are more precious to the Father than you know."

Matthew: "I feel a special uneasiness. Being a former tax collector has not endeared me to many."

Jesus: "Don't let your past destroy your present and cloud your future. Listen to what I am telling you, Matthew. Listen, all of you. The real enemy is the one who can kill your soul. The real enemy is the one who can sap your zeal and shrink your imagination. The real enemy is the one who plants the seeds of self-doubt and self-pity. Pick up your cross and follow me in the work of the Kingdom. And even if you should lose your life for my sake, have hope and confidence that you will gain it to life eternal. It is time to go."

Jesus sent the twelve disciples off with strong words and a silent prayer for their ministry. Jesus knew well how innocent and inexperienced they were. There would be many challenges and crosses; exciting opportunities and depressing set-backs. All of these are part of the ministry of the Kingdom and the following of Jesus. In time, they would be calling and sending forth others in the name of Jesus through the power of the Kingdom. Down through the centuries, disciples would continue to teach in the name of Jesus. In the face of opposition and hostility and indifference, they would proclaim the good news of salvation and teach the mysteries of the Kingdom of God.

The Golden Age is a Golden Calf

The pilgrim aspect of the Church involves us in the mystery of time and time is a mystery. St. Augustine once wrote that he knew what time was until asked, then he did not know. We often try to solve the mystery of time in two ways: we advance to the past and idealize some time not our own. The "mythic chords of memory" filter out the uncomfortable and the sinful. Memory retains what is desired and elevates it to a moment of absolute revelation. The other strategy is to rush fast forward into the future. The utopian drive is strong, especially in the west. The idea of progress drives not only science and technology, but religion as well. Tomorrow *must* be better than today and certainly an improvement over yesterday. Why? For no other reason than it is a time not yet. Both strategies share one thing in common: a rejection of the present. The present is rejected because it does not measure up to the golden past. The present is trivialized in terms of the perfection that is about to be.

The mystery of time cannot be solved by escaping to the past or reaching into the future. As the Bible tells us — now is the acceptable time and moment of our salvation. It is the present which holds the past and leads to the future. It is in the present that God breaks into our hearts and speaks his word.

The mystery of time is not a problem to be solved but a fundamental characteristic of being human and being a community of faith. The mystery of time requires the grace of courage. Paul Tillich, in his sermon, "The Eternal Now," preached the following:

> . . . every moment of time reaches into the eternal. It is the eternal that stops the flux of time for us. It is the eternal "now" which provides for us a temporal "now" . . . not everybody, and nobody all the time, is aware of this "eternal now" in the temporal "now." But sometimes it breaks powerfully into our consciousness and gives us the certainty of the eternal, of a dimension of time which cuts into time and gives us our time . . . People who are never aware of this dimension (the eternal now) lose the possibility of resting in the present . . . They are held by the past and cannot separate themselves from it, or they escape towards the future, unable to rest in the present . . . Perhaps this is the most conspicuous characteristic of our period . . . It lacks the courage to accept "presence" because it has lost the dimension of the eternal . . . There is *one* power that surpasses the all-consuming power of time — the eternal; He Who was and is and is to come, the beginning and the end. He gives us forgiveness for what has passed. He gives us courage for what is to come. He gives us rest in His eternal Presence.
>
> (*The Eternal Now*)

The Church is that community of faith caught in that mysterious suspension of time. In times of transition, the temptation is great to return to a safe and more comfortable historical moment. For example, the Israelites were liberated from bondage in Egypt. However, life in the wilderness left a great deal to be desired. The community soon began to murmur against Moses and Aaron: "Would that we died by the hand of the Lord in the land of Egypt, when we sat by the fleshpots and ate bread to the full; for you have brought us out into this wilderness to kill this whole assembly with hunger" (Ex 16:3). Life in Egypt looked more appealing than life in the wilderness as the way to the promised land. The past had killed the present and obstructed the future. The temptation is always at hand to judge the whole by one of its parts. We reject our wilderness present in terms of some past glory. We escape our difficult "now" by rushing uncritically into a future of our own designs. We modern Israelites do our share of murmuring as we wander in the contemporary wilderness. Often we seek a return to some golden age in the Church which provided a sure identity and a high level of security. However, such a return is both unrealistic and unfaithful to the pilgrim appeal of the Church. Above all, such a return bespeaks a lack of hope. The renowned theologian Hans Urs von Balthasar writes:

> The life of the Church is like walking on the spot; it is journeying in the darkness of faith . . . which renders vain all calculations of progress. The constantly self-realizing point of intersection between transient time and salvation time causes the duration of the Church to appear as an ever-present dramatic event which, precisely because of the indwelling of the eternal in it, can never be seen as a whole . . . To be in historical time means to journey in a foreign land. Not because God has not providentially impregnated everything with his presence, but because the form of temporality itself, by its lack of unity, is an absence of the creature from unified eternity.
>
> (*Man in History*)

The provisional and pilgrimage aspects of the Church provide us with a crucial lesson, namely, that heaven and earth will pass away but the word of the Lord abides. The present order is always imperfect *and always incomplete*. God's judgment critiques all the works of our hands and finds them wanting. All of our knowledge will pass away. Our prophesying will cease. Our dogmas and doctrines can never fully express the inexpressible mystery who is God. The liturgy we celebrate, the faith we hold, and the virtue we practice are all straw when compared to the unsurpassing knowledge and experience of our Lord Jesus Christ. The life of the Church and

Church life are important for our salvation. But they are important as means to the one, ultimate end who is God. The God who is the final good of our journey is always present throughout, calling us to ever greater degrees of faith, hope, and love.

We need to look backward in order to appreciate the labors of our ancestors in faith and the work of the God who is faithful to his promises. This backward glance is done more in gratitude than in longing. We have no desire to return to that time which is not our own yet continues to abide in our present. We look forward with a confident hope that the One who was faithful will complete the good work he has begun in us this day. Simply put, we are a community of faith which journeys in time knowing that all time is toward home.

Once again we focus our eye on that distant mirror of the first century. We look backward in gratitude to our ancestors in faith, Paul, Timothy, and Titus. They have much to teach us. Again, we do not look backward in order to simply copy what they said and did. Rather, we look for their guidance so that *in our own time* we may respond to the Spirit with the same fidelity, creativity, and courage. The dust of time is gently wiped aside. We see our three ancestors in deep discussion. As we draw closer, the following conversation unfolds:

Timothy: "Tell me, Paul, are teachers born or made?"

Paul: "Teachers are underpaid! Just kidding. I am not sure that teaching is a question of nature or nurture. It has more to do with the Holy Spirit. The really good teachers are alive in the Spirit. The really bad teachers are so dull they even test the Holy Ghost."

Timothy: "I really like to teach but I must admit I am having a difficult time with some of my students. They are very much attracted to some teachers who offer them myths and genealogies."

Paul: "These teachers also touch their imagination. This is very powerful for any teacher. In fact,

	touching the imagination is crucial for good teaching."
Timothy:	"Are you taking up for these so-called teachers at Ephesus? I would think you would find their work deplorable."
Paul:	"You know I am not taking up for them! What I am asking you to do, Timothy, is to be wise and mature enough to learn from everyone, yes, even these teachers whom you don't find acceptable. God uses us to do his work. God takes everything and tries to bring some good to pass. These teachers are touching the imagination."
Timothy:	"How do I go about such teaching? Maybe I don't have such an ability to get the message across."
Paul:	"Once again, you need to realize that teaching is a blending of our human personality and the gift of grace. Both are needed. Remember nothing attracts the imagination like the truth. Good teaching involves not simply clear and distinct ideas, but also stories, symbols, images, paintings, music, and architecture. You must learn, as a teacher, to connect the head to the heart."
Titus:	"I've had my share of difficulty with students and teachers who are upsetting a good number of Cretans. So many people are involved in idle speculation and simply engage in useless debate. Why don't people just believe and behave?"
Paul:	"I am not sure we would want blind obedience. Unthinking adherence is just as dangerous as those who foster controversy just for its shock value. Not everyone who teaches what we consider novel is trying to gain popularity or tickle the ears of students. Questions are not a sign of rebellion. They can be the highest form of respect. The motivation of teaching and questioning is crucial."

Titus: "That's a very difficult thing to judge — motivation. We can easily be deceived."

Paul: "And we can easily deceive. Look, Titus, none of this is easy. The Master and Teacher told us that by the fruits we produce we come to know about our motivation. Eventually we reap what we sow."

Timothy: "So far we have just been discussing methods or styles. The real problem is with teaching sound doctrine."

Paul: "Unfortunately, we too quickly dismiss method and style. We need to remember that our sound teaching comes in a human being. We ought not to minimize the medium who brings the message. But certainly sound doctrine is very important."

Timothy: "It seems that people have rejected the Gospel and doctrine in order to do their own thing."

Titus: "I know what you mean. Too often, my students want to change this doctrine or alter that teaching. We can't simply build our own doctrine from scratch. That would be chaos."

Paul: "A good principle that has served me in teaching is this: *everything up to a point*. When we go beyond a certain point, then we are being unfaithful. At a certain point, we are no longer in the community of faith."

Titus: "And what is that point?"

Paul: "Wouldn't you be bored if I told you? This point is not something we measure mathematically. It requires prayer, prudence, participation by the whole community, and the wisdom to discern spirits. We know how easy it is to claim the Spirit has sent us, taught us, and told us. We can't expect more certainty than is reasonable. As hard as it is for us to tolerate, we must learn to live with a certain amount of tension and ambiguity."

Timothy: "Isn't that a major problem for the community? I
               mean this ambiguity causes confusion and many
               to doubt their faith. We must be certain
               trumpets."

Paul: "Perhaps you don't trust the Holy Spirit and the
               good sense of the community. At times, the
               Spirit works from the community upward. Good
               teachers are also good learners. It is more than a
               little arrogant to believe that the Spirit speaks
               only through us. I realize now how much I have
               learned from the communities I have taught.
               Once upon a time, I would never have admitted
               that."

Timothy: "I must say this, Paul. It seems that you are
               weakening our authority. Won't people lose re-
               spect for us and the message?"

Paul: "Let's make an important distinction between
               the authoritarian and the authoritative. Great
               damage is done by an authoritarian approach to
               teaching and preaching. It is easy to confuse
               such an approach with strength and being
               moral. In reality, it reveals a great weakness,
               lack of respect for those whom we serve, and
               gives evidence of little faith. By contrast, the
               authoritative respects human freedom and
               reason. The authoritative knows the human has
               limits, as well, and hence is always open to and
               dependent upon grace. Authoritative teaching
               invites, lures, beckons, and challenges hearts to
               be changed by the power of the Spirit rather than
               the force of fear which in the end fails and is
               rejected by Jesus as belonging to Caesar."

Titus: "I can see this is a very important distinction."

Timothy: "I, too, can see what you are saying. At times, I
               feel I must teach as hard, or harder, than those
               on the other side."

Paul: "This is the dynamic of extremism and the first thing to be sacrificed is the truth of the Gospel. In effect, the other side wins because the authentic Gospel of Jesus is not being taught. The Gospel is not meant to be a burden, but a great joy which brings life in abundance."

Titus: "Paul, we just get down at times and it seems we double the effort. Unfortunately, we can fail to see the goal."

Paul: "Good teaching requires you to be men of prayer. Remember, you are not teaching angels or beasts. You are teaching human beings like yourselves. We are all earthen vessels. We carry a great treasure — the Spirit — within as well. Prayer will help you in your teaching ministry. You will be faithful to the Gospel. You will teach sound doctrine in such a way that minds will become open to wisdom. And you will teach with love so that all will know you are a true disciple of the Lord Jesus Christ."

This lively discussion continued for some time. In fact, it endures throughout the centuries and will do so until Christ comes again in glory. Each new generation must respectfully and gratefully receive the Gospel and the living tradition of the community of faith. The Gospel and tradition are received with the obligation to be good stewards, that is, we are to grow deeper into its mysteries. We are to hand on to those who follow what we have received, along with our struggles and joys concerning the mysteries ever old and ever new. It is to our present situation that we now turn our attention. It is to the present conversation that we want to add our voices.

Faith Today

The doing of theology (community God-talk) always requires a number of qualifiers. God-talk, theology, is always done through a given culture, society, historical epoch, tradi-

tion, language, and human personality. In other words, our
God-talk is a very fragile and limited endeavor. There is
always an incompleteness and inadequacy in our speaking of
things divine. Hence, we always receive from the past frag-
ments and clippings of the really real. We add our own frag-
ments and insights as we wrestle with the Spirit in our time. We
pass on to those who come after us a larger, richer, but in no
way complete, story of God. We would be idolatrous to conclude that we have in our intellectual barns all we need in order
to know the Lord. We are now able to rest and take it easy.
Jesus warned that the Father may requires our very souls this
night. The doing of theology requires each new generation to
read the signs of the time.

What is happening today? What are the signs of the time
which are at work qualifying our God-talk? What challenges
are present as we continue the past and present ministry and
mission of teaching? Naturally, no list would be complete or
comprehensive. The reading of our historical situation is incomplete and we see through a glass darkly. Yet we must
continue to look at old and familiar things with new eyes. In the
image of the unknown poet in Isaiah, we must not grow weary
or faint but search for the Lord who renews our strength, who
helps us to see the things on high.

1. To borrow from the sociology of knowledge (Peter L.
Berger), our present situation is one that is devoid of a "sacred
canopy." The Catholic-Christian world view no longer domi-
nates the cultural symbols of what is true, beautiful, and good.
We live in a time which evidences a "multiplicity of plausibility structures." There are a number of competing definitions of
reality and what is worthy of our time and attention. Today, the
major "reality policemen" are found among the scientific community. Father Karl Rahner, S.J. writes:

> We are living in a world in which the general conscious-
> ness of society and of each individual is fundamentally
> and deeply stamped by the sciences, that is, by the
> historical sciences which, despite their function of sum-

ming up general trends, tend to make historical realities
relatives, by the autonomous, exact, and functional
natural sciences and by the empirical social services
thinking likewise in almost the same terms.

(*The Shape of the Church to Come*)

This shift from a single sacred canopy to a multiplicity of
plausibility structures dominated by science affects the Christian in the marketplace. There is no longer the taken-for-
granted aspect of faith. We no longer enjoy the homogeneous
structures, within and outside of the Church, which confirm
identity and support one in time on the way to eternity. The
Christian must be more involved in making a free, informed,
and often counter-cultural decision to follow the way of the
Lord. Some bemoan the waning of the Christian culture. Yet
might we not also see this dying as a new birth for a faith which
calls for a decision against the currents? The decision for God
requires a personal decision to leave our cultural nets and
follow him. The cost of discipleship requires that the grace of a
homogeneous culture and faith *not* be ours. Our spirituality
and teaching will be done in a new situation. Again, Father
Rahner:

The spirituality of the future will not be supported or at
any rate will be much less supported by a sociologically
Christian homogeneity of its situation; it will have to live
much more clearly than hitherto and of a solitary, immediate experience of God and his Spirit in the individual . . . In such a situation the lonely responsibility of
the individual in his decision of faith is necessary and
required in a way much more radical than it was in former
times. That is why the modern spirituality of the Christian
involves courage for solitary decision contrary to public
opinion, the lovely courage analogous to that of the
martyrs of the first century of Christianity, the courage for
a spiritual decision of faith, drawing its strength from
itself and not needing to be supported by public agreement, particularly since even the Church's public opin-

ion does not so much sustain the individual in his decision of faith, but is sustained by the latter. Such a solitary
courage, however, can exist only if it lives out of a wholly
personal experience of God and his spirit.

(Concern for the Church)

2. This new situation (which really connects with the
situation of our first century ancestors in faith) of faith is
reflective of the new situation in western culture as a whole.
Many of the changes in the life of the Church are reflective of
the changes in culture. Jesuit philosopher and theologian,
Father Bernard Lonergan, S.J., has characterized the shift in
culture as the change from a classical to a modern culture.

The classical culture comes by way of ancient Greece.
The predominant values of the classical culture emphasized
the immutable, eternal, fixed, and universal aspects of reality.
The Christian religion expressed itself within these cultural
resources. God is the Prime Mover and First Cause who lives in
unapproachable light ordering all things to their ends, but
remaining unmoved by their actions. The Church and the
whole of life on earth were likewise viewed in very fixed
categories. Such a view of reality provided a great deal of
security as well as a very strong sense of identity and destiny.
This type of world view, however, is limited by certain beliefs:
that all change is negative; that history contains little, if any,
value; and that diversity is but another name for chaos. The
classical culture always runs the risk of passing from un-
iformity to conformity and, finally, to an aggressive intolerance
towards those who are different. Also, a religion too closely
connected with a given cultural expression can easily become
a widow as the culture shifts to a new form.

By contrast, the modern cultural world view is characterized by change, flux, pluralism, and the rise of historical
consciousness. The influence of science places a great deal of
importance on the senses, human experience, and empirical
verification through the methods of science. There is no one
sacred canopy which defines what is true, beautiful, and good.

There are many ways to express the Christian life. No one form is normative to the exclusion of others. The clashing of ideas, experiences, structures, values, and beliefs are looked upon in a positive way. In fact, such a dialectical aspect enhances life and helps us to understand the richness of human existence (and faith as well). The dangers from such a cultural world view are obvious: individualism, subjectivism, and relativism. In time, all reality becomes reduced to that which can be known *only* by the methods of science. The metaphysical and the imaginative-speculative aspects of the mind and heart are trivialized or ignored. There is no objective, perennial truth, but mere opinion which changes with the times and the culture. Theologian Michael Novak expresses the limitations of the modern cultural way of judging faith and forming morals as follows:

> . . . knowledge in matters of faith and morals, unlike knowledge in modern sciences, has a remarkable constancy, even in the clearer light of new distinctions and new methods . . . in medicine and other modern scientific work, new breakthroughs into the unknown occur constantly; in the humanities, by contrast, movement is rather from the known to the more accurately known. . . . The sciences constantly overturn earlier scientific classics. Humanists constantly cite the humanistic classics for evidence that they are on the right track, still retaining their indispensable universality.

Professor Novak also uncovers the danger of historical consciousness, that is, the belief that all is relative and nothing is perennial or universal.

> Historical consciousness is a relatively new discovery . . . historical consciousness must not be surrendered to historicism, in which there lies *nothing but* a "diversity of approaches based on historical and cultural differences." That way lies pure relativism. If the human mind is not capable of rising above the subjectivity of individual thinkers and the prejudices of the spirit of the times, then

fidelity to God's word is impossible across the ages, and philosophers can enjoy no real communion across cultures and down the centuries. Even "the development of doctrine" would then be only an illusion. ("Dissent in the Church," *Vatican Authority and American Catholic Dissent*, edited by Wm. W. May.)

Catholic theology is carried on in this modern cultural context with its profound achievements and dangerous shallowness. Theology requires a great degree of cooperation and mutual respect between bishop and theologian. Such is all the more important since the theologian enjoys a greater degree of freedom than was allowed in former times and the bishop is involved more in administrative than in direct theological concerns. There is a mutual need at work as well for mutual trust. However, sin (distrust) is no respecter of persons — bishop and theologian included. As Father Edward K. Braxton writes, in his excellent book, *The Wisdom Community*, "theologians can be arrogant and self-seeking and bishops can be authoritarian and defensive." While it is all too easy to assume, especially given the media attention directed to debate and dissent in the Catholic Church, that *all* bishops live in the thirteenth century and *all* theologians are writing the documents for Vatican III, such is not the case. In fact, as Father Braxton rightly observes, "Each is solicitous for the good of the Church. Each is further aware that the great bishop-theologians of the past were also saints!"

To teach with authority and to pastor as good shepherds, we need to keep ever before us the call to holiness and sanctity. In a world come of age, such a reminder might seem like pious sentiment; ideology in the service of religious authority; or a call to obey and fall in line. None of the above is intended. Rather, the call to holiness is the ground of every vocation, calling, and service in the Church. There is no such thing as a call to serve which does not first acknowledge the call to holiness. Great teachers realize how much they learn at the *prie-dieu* as well as at the word processor. Good shepherds know that they can only lead the community to the Good Shepherd if they are men of personal holiness. Catholic theology holds that there is no conflict between faith and reason. The same can be said for scholarship and sanctity.

Two great minds of the Catholic tradition are St. Thomas Aquinas and John Henry Cardinal Newman. They were also men of prayer and holiness. As we bring this section to a close, prayerfully consider the prayers of these great men of mind and holiness.

Creator, beyond any words of ours to describe!
Most gloriously have you disposed all parts of the whole universe.
You are the true source of light and wisdom, you are their first and final cause.
Pour out now, I beg you, a ray of your clear light upon my murky understanding, and take from me my doubly dark inheritance of sin and ignorance. You who inspire the speech of little children, guide and teach my tongue now, and let the grace of your blessing flow upon my lips. Grant me a sharp discernment, a strong memory, a methodical approach to study, a willing and able docility; let me be precise in interpretation and felicitous in choice of words.
Instruct my beginning, direct my progress, and bring my work to its proper finish: You, who are true God and true Man, living and reigning forever!

— St. Thomas Aquinas

Come, O my dear Lord, and teach me in like manner. I need it not, and do not ask it, as far as this, that the word of truth which in the beginning was given to the Apostles by thee, has been handed down from age to age, and has already been taught to me, and thy infallible Church is the warrant of it. But I need thee to teach me day by day, according to each day's opportunities and needs. I need thee to give me that true driving instinct about revealed matters that, knowing one part, I may be able to anticipate or to approve of others. I need that understanding of the truths about thyself which may prepare me for all thy other truths — or at least may save me from conjecturing falsely upon them. I need the mind of the Spirit, which is the mind of the holy Fathers, and of the Church by which I may not only say what they say on definite points, but think what they think; in all I need to be saved from an originality of thought, which is not true if it leads away from thee. Give me the gift of discriminating between true and false in all discourse of mine.

                              — John Henry Cardinal Newman

3. The winds of modernity (some might say the acids) have not only affected those in chancery, pulpit, and academy. The winds of change are blowing strongly among those in the pew. The immigrant Church of the late nineteenth and mid-twentieth centuries has passed away. In place of the immigrant Church is what Eugene Kennedy calls "the Space Age Church." Among its characteristics the following bear mentioning: the role of the laity has been expanded; leadership can no longer rely on simply giving orders and must build consensus; a renewed interest in social justice; and the need to engage in ecumenical dialogue. While all of these exert great influence on the teaching ministry of the Church, the following is most crucial: the Catholic population has made tremendous advances in both education and occupational status in the years following the Second Vatican Council. The implications of such changes are hard to overstate. Father Andrew Greeley, a sociologist of the first order, in his study of the American laity, writes:

> The years since the end of the Second Vatican Council have been marked by profound and accelerating economic and occupational changes among American Catholics, changes so massive and so sweeping that no serious reflection on the condition of American Catholics can afford to forget even for a moment that the religious change related to the Second Vatican Council came at the

same time that economic and occupational changes were sweeping American Catholics ahead of white Protestants' economic achievement. Moreover, planning for the future of the American Catholic Church must take into account the fact that economic and occupational change has not ended and will not end before the beginning of the next century. It is likely to go on at even more rapid a pace in the next two decades than it did in the past two decades. (*American Catholics Since the Council*)

Father Andrew Greeley has performed a consistent and high quality service for the Church throughout his various sociological studies of Catholic life in America. Whether one agrees or disagrees with his conclusions or interpretations is beside the point. What is to the point is this: no one who is concerned about the present and future Church in America can afford to ignore his studies. They provide us with much needed empirical data and sociological correlations between belief and action; role and behavior; authority and obedience; religious imagination and Catholic practice. In terms of the changing educational and occupational advances within the Catholic community, the following points are crucial:

- In contrast to the past, the Catholic population which is maturing in the 1980's is attending college in significant numbers. Not only are Catholics "catching up" with Protestants in terms of college attendance, but they are even surpassing the Protestant population. The years ahead will see Catholics attend in even greater numbers.
- Catholics are not only attending college in greater numbers than in years past, but are increasing their presence in the professional and managerial spheres of work. Again, Catholics are outdistancing their Protestant counterparts in occupational achievement.
- Naturally, if Catholics are attending college and working in the professional and managerial spheres, their income is bound to rise. In the early 1980's, American Catholics earned $1,000.00 per year more than white Methodists,

$3,000.00 per year more than white Lutherans, and
$5,000.00 per year more than white Baptists. However,
Catholics trail white Presbyterians by $3,000.00, white
Episcopalians by $8,000.00, and Jews by $10,000.00.

(For a detailed analysis of Catholics in America, see Father
Greeley's works, *The American Catholic: A Social Portrait*; *The
Education of Catholic Americans*; and *American Catholics
Since the Council.*)

The implications for Catholic leadership and the ministry
of teaching are far-reaching. American Catholics are no longer
simply willing to believe and behave. Catholics want to know
the reasons for their faith and moral values. The ministry of
pastor and teacher can no longer be carried on with a simple,
"because father or the bishop says so." There are "gathering
storms in the Catholic Church" (Jeffrey K. Haydden) in terms
of the growing disparity between pulpit and pew in terms of
education. Unlike years gone by, it is the laity who are often
better educated and more professionally trained than priests.
With an increased attendance at college, a rising occupational
status, and more money, the average Catholic in America is
more independent. A growing number of Catholics are remaining Catholic *on their own terms*. Some have called this "communal Catholicism," "selective Catholicism," "cafeteria
Catholicism,' or "erector-set Catholicism." Others do not see
this approach as Catholicism at all! Regardless, the Catholic in
the pew has changed over the past several decades. He or she
is better educated, more professionally trained, enjoys an
increased income, highly independent, questioning, at times
angry, and fiercely determined to remain Catholic. The data
indicates this generation of Catholics will not go away. Hence,
the real challenge has passed to those in leadership positions
of teacher and shepherd. Once again, the challenge is at hand
to prepare a new generation of Catholics; a generation which is
as exciting and committed as it is new.

By What Authority?

The twentieth chapter of Luke's Gospel opens with Jesus "teaching the people in the temple and preaching the Gospel." The officials of established religion took offense at Jesus' ministry. After all, this was a carpenter's son and he did not have a diploma which would certify as to his competence. The chief priests and the scribes and elders confronted Jesus with this, "Tell us by what authority you do these things, or who it is that gave you this authority?" (Lk 20:2). Their request endures down through the centuries to our own time and no doubt will continue to do so until the Lord comes to provide the definitive answer. Until then, we must continue to provide an answer for our hope and our authority for teaching, preaching, and ministry. Lutheran pastor Richard John Neuhaus provides us with some wise insights worthy of long consideration:

> . . . any ministry that finds its authority in contemporary notions of professionalism is on perilous ground indeed. Yet the walls of many clergy offices are littered by diplomas and certificates from academic institutions and professional associations . . . shoddy evidence of authorization . . . The appeal to the appurtenances of professionalism is a poignant confession of vocational bankruptcy . . . If the wall of the pastor's office is to make a declaration worthy of the calling, let it display a simple cross or crucifix. That, finally, is all we have to say for ourselves. Upon that cross and the community of resurrection faith gathered around that cross our commitment stands or falls. That is the insecurity that is at the very heart of our freedom. That insecurity cannot be relieved — we should not want it to be — by a letter from corporate headquarters or a certification from a professional association. (*Freedom for Ministry*)

In the final analysis, the source of the authority to teach is the person of Jesus Christ. This is not said in order to silence questions or to withdraw behind a neat religious slogan. It is an awesome thing to proclaim the word of the Lord and to teach in his name. The mighty often reject such a word and authority as a challenge to their might and comfortable seats of power. To ground one's authority in Jesus is to be one with the Man of Sorrows who cries from the Cross, "My God, my God, why have you forsaken me?" To teach in the shadow of the Cross is to offer lessons that many consider stumbling blocks and folly. Shepherds seem like fools to the wise and mighty who trust in the works of their hands. Shepherds boldly proclaim a foolishness which in reality is the very power of salvation and the true hope of mankind.

The Church which proclaims Jesus as Lord; the Church which can count among its members Augustine, Thomas, Francis, Scholastica, and Catherine; the Church which has sent into a hurting world a Vincent de Paul, Dorothy Day, and Mother Teresa, is a Church richly blessed in wisdom and love. We have our own problems and possibilities. But we continue to proclaim our faith in light of a blessed heritage and a confident hope in the God who is Truth and Love. Bishops and theologians must be men and women of the Shepherd and teach with authority — the authority of Jesus Christ. The closing will be left to a great Protestant pastor and theologian, Reinhold Niebuhr. His words can offer a new opportunity to teach with authority:

> The wisdom by which we deal with our fellow men, either as comrades or competitors, is not so much an intellectual achievement as the fruit of a humility which is gained by prayer. The faith through which we understand the meaning of our existence and the fulfillment of that meaning in the divine mercy is, ultimately, a gift of grace and not the consequence of a sophisticated analysis of the signs of the times. We are not merely minds, but total personalities. We can deal with immediate issues as personalities. And we deal with them truly only if, not the ignorance of the mind, but the pride of the heart has been vanquished. (*Discerning the Signs of the Times*)

IV

THE MORAL LIFE:
Narrative, Community, and Virtue

Consider the following all too common exchange between Jane and her bewildered mother. Before we get to the dialogue, a word of introduction concerning our characters is called for. Jane is a pretty, popular, and intelligent sixteen-year-old. She attends Catholic school and even goes to church on Sunday. Her teachers find her appealing and a "good leader."

Jane's mother, Helen, is a stay-at-home mom. She watches, and is often shocked, at what takes place on Donahue. Helen is happily married and has good communication with Jane (her only daughter). Yet there are times when Helen wonders "about Jane's morals." This concern is especially felt in areas of sexual morality. Teenage pregnancy, the fear of AIDS, and the general lack of permanence in human relationships are issues of great concern for parents and high interest for adolescents. While Helen believes that Jane is "a good girl," at times she wonders if she and Jack (her husband) have done a good job as parents preparing Jane for "the outside world."

We now turn to a recent dinner table conversation between Jane and Helen. Jack was out of town on a business trip. Jane wanted to do something special for her mother, so she prepared the meal. It was Helen who would provide the main course in terms of dinner conversation. It went something like this:

Helen: "I can't believe some of the topics which are discussed on those talk shows in the morning. Just this morning, a panel of parents and so-called experts were talking about teenage pregnancy and premarital sex."

Jane: "What were some of the things they said?"

Helen: "Most of their talking expressed concern about the rising rate of teenage pregnancy. However, their solution was unbelievable. They suggested a massive program on sexual education."

Jane: "What's wrong with that? The trouble is too many young people don't know the facts of life."

Helen: "Honey, most of the sex education is in terms of how to avoid getting pregnant. And naturally you avoid getting pregnant by using the pill or some other device."

Jane: "Well, mother, the pill does prevent pregnancy."

Helen: "Did it ever occur to you that the best way to avoid pregnancy is to abstain from sex in the first place?"

Jane: "Sex and love go together. When you really love someone, you want to give yourself to him. Isn't that so?"

Helen: "Not always. Sex and love *might* go together. However, sex can be used or misused in a number of ways. Sex can be a sign of power, control, or a simple escape. Besides, sex is reserved only for marriage."

Jane: "Why? Do you mean that *all* people who are married really love one another? Do you mean that every act of sex between husband and wife is pure love?"

Helen: "Of course not. Not every act of sex, even in marriage, is an act of pure love. Husbands and wives can do very unloving things to one another. Yet you shouldn't judge marriage by its failures. After all, Jane, we don't reject medicine just because the patient dies."

Jane: "Mother, what matters is that two people love each other. They can stay together and give to one another as long as they feel love for one another."

Helen: "What happens when they don't feel like loving anymore? What happens when someone else comes along with a better offer?"

Jane: "Things are not like they once were. Today, we're much more open and free about sex and relationships. We try to trust one another more."

Helen: "What about the sacrament of marriage? Didn't they teach you in school that marriage is holy and sex is only for a married couple?"

Jane: "Yes. But . . ."

Helen: "But what? Don't you realize the damage done by people who sleep around? This damage is worse for females. It is the girl who holds all the negatives. She has to take the pill. She has to have the abortion. She has to raise the child. It is the girl who must often withdraw from school and begin her life as a mother — a single mother! So much for your trust and equality!"

Jane: "It doesn't always work out that way. If you really love the other person, you are very careful. It seems *you* are judging the situation by its failures. I know girls who are very happy living with their boyfriends. They didn't need a wedding or some ceremony."

Helen: "Is this really what you believe is right? Is this what we have taught you all these years? What about your Catholic training? Have we all failed?"

Jane: "Of course not. Why do you think you failed? We just don't agree on something. It doesn't mean you failed or that I am wrong. We just have different viewpoints. Why can't we just agree to disagree?"

Helen: "We are not disagreeing about toothpaste or on what we are having for dinner. We are talking about morals and values. I can't believe that you would live with a boy before you are married."

Jane: "Mother, I didn't say that I would do that. I just said that I could understand others doing that. We can't force our values on others. Everyone has to make up her own mind about how she feels. What's so bad about that?"

Helen: "What's so bad? There are just some things that we cannot simply choose to obey or not obey. The moral law, the Commandments, are not the Ten Suggestions."

Jane: "I respect you and what you feel. Why can't you do the
same? I don't think you are a bad person because you
disagree with me. I just have different feelings than
you do."

Helen: "Morality is not about feelings! You have to obey what
God wants of us. To have sex outside of marriage is to
violate God's law."

Jane: "Who says this is God's law?"

Helen: "The Church. You are a member of the Catholic
Church. There are rules and regulations. You simply
can't do whatever you want to do."

Jane: "Mother, I am not sure that we are getting anywhere.
You have your beliefs and I have mine. Why don't we
leave it at that?"

The above conversation highlights the current situation in
moral discourse, namely, that there is a lack of shared fundamental beliefs about the moral life. The division and discord
are not merely generational. They are not limited to issues of
sexual ethics. Across the ethical spectrum, we find ourselves
without a shared language and narrative by which we make
moral decisions. Even more troubling, we lack consensus
about fundamental principles so as to be able to carry on a
rational disagreement. Too often, we find ourselves simply
asserting our beliefs, prejudices, or feelings. The other person
(opponent) then asserts his feelings and we find ourselves at a
standoff. We resolve nothing and advance not one step in the
way of truth. In the end, moral belief and values are held to be
valid if we feel them intensely and sincerely. Validity is
proportional to the intensity of sincerity. In the final analysis,
moral issues are settled by the Gallup Poll, media visibility,
and the ability to put one's supporters on the streets. Objective
truth gives way to emotive assertions about one's subjective
values and beliefs.

Professor Alasdair MacIntyre, in his brilliant book, *After
Virtue*, understands the chaos of our present moral situation in
terms of emotivism. That is, our actions are guided by our

feelings. And feelings are nothing but expressions of our attitudes and subjective states. Hence, all values are private and cannot be challenged by objective criteria and the faculty of human reason. The result is a standoff in which we are, in the words of our young friend Jane, "Not sure we are getting anywhere." We are simply left with our feelings. Professor MacIntyre writes:

> The most striking feature of contemporary moral utterance is that so much of it is used to express disagreements; and the most striking feature of the debates in which these disagreements are expressed is their interminable character. I do not mean by this just that such debates go on and on and on — although they do — but also that they apparently can find no terminus. There seems to be no rational way of securing moral agreement in our culture. (*After Virtue*)

The realization that we lack a shared foundation for our beliefs and values causes anxiety, not only for Helen, but for all of us. We find ourselves hard-pressed to give a reason for our hope and a rational framework for our beliefs and values. We find ourselves retreating into the private world of feeling. In so doing, we deny the status of truth to values and beliefs. Values and religious beliefs are nothing more than subjective expressions of our inner feelings, and religious beliefs are not convictions but preferences. To borrow a phrase from Karl Marx, "all that is solid melts into air." We are thrown on our own to erect our own private moral universe. We have become like gods. We must construct the world of values. Yet, in our more reflective moments (those moments when we know we are just clay), we experience a great anxiety and self-doubt. For if we have made and chosen these values, can't we unmake and discard them? The moral world is human, all too human, and all too fragile to sustain us individuals as a community. The fragility of the moral life is insightfully captured by Professor Stanley Hauerwas:

I suspect that the experience of the world as morally adrift
has a more profound source than the mere observation
that people are permitted to do what was once unthink-
able. Our disquiet about morality more likely arises from
within us. Even though we feel strongly about abortion,
divorce, dishonesty, and so on, we are not sure why we
feel as we do. And the less sure we are of the reason for
our beliefs, the more dogmatically we hold them as our
only still point in a morally chaotic world . . . the very
notion we are "choosing" or "making up" our morality
contains the seeds of its own destruction, for moral authenticity seems to require that morality be not a matter of
one's own shaping, but something that shapes me. We do
not create moral values, principles, virtues; rather they
constitute a life for us to appropriate.

(*The Peaceable Kingdom*)

How do we as Catholic Christians live morally and faithfully in a world which appears to be morally adrift and spiritu-
ally indifferent (or hostile)? The temptation is great to claim a
special immunity because we rely on God's will or Church
teachings or some special religious experience. At the other
end of the temptation spectrum is the modern attraction to
cultural relativism. Religious values and beliefs are made to
conform to the current cultural expressions of reality. In time,
it becomes hard, if not impossible, to distinguish between
religious beliefs and values and what a given culture holds to
be true, beautiful, and good. Both temptations must be rejected, for we quickly come to see how fragile the foundation is
on which they rest. We as Christians want neither immunity
from ambiguity nor fellowship with a culture that quickly
passes away. What is at stake is the question of truth: are our
religious beliefs and moral virtues true? We Christians search
for the truth which liberates; the truth which is not the work of
our hands but a gift of grace; the truth which is the way to
eternal life. This cannot be emphasized enough: *THE CHRIS-
TIAN MORAL LIFE IS GROUNDED IN THE PERSON OF
JESUS. HOW WE RESPOND TO THE PERSON OF JESUS*

*DETERMINES WHO WE ARE. OUR CHRISTIAN BELIEFS
ARE ONE WITH OUR MORALITY.*

We Catholics are used to thinking about and doing ethics
in terms of rules, principles, regulations, and judging the
objective morality of individual acts. All of these things are
important for the moral life. Yet there is something prior to
these, namely, the question of identity. Before we ask the
question, "What are we to do?", the moral identity (character)
of the person is evidenced in the actions in which one engages.
We are known by what we do, and what we do proceeds from
who we are. Wayne A. Meeks, in his excellent study of the
origins of the Christian life, *The Moral World of the First
Christians*, writes:

> We tend to think of ethics as moral argument or rules. We
> live in a culture of experts, in which there are profes-
> sional ethicists who are experts in the construction of
> arguments and the analysis of rules . . . This is ethics
> from the top down.

> There is, however, a way of looking at ethics from the
> bottom up, in which it is a perfectly proper form of ethical
> directive to say, for example to a child, "We do not do
> that." Probably the response from the child and perhaps
> also from the professional ethicist, will be, "Why not?"
> Very often that is an important question to ask, but there
> are other occasions when it may be more productive to
> ask a different question: Who are "we"? The question
> "Why?" calls for an explanation; "Who?" invites
> understanding.

It is to this "Who?", who we are as a people, that we now
turn our attention. In order to properly address this question of
identity (who?) as a way into *what* we are to do, we look to
Jesus. The Christian life is that daily process of telling *our*
personal stories in loving, obedient union with the story of
Jesus. We must come to know the person of Jesus and what he
is offering us as the truth and the life. We must learn to tell our
story within the larger story of Jesus of Nazareth.

Jesus: The Message of the Kingdom

By all accounts, it was an ordinary day. For Palestine, the ordinary could be kindly described as chaotic. (Chaos in the Middle East is not a new story.) The Romans were in charge and those chosen to rule on the local level were answerable to Caesar. The air was thick with political talk about driving the Romans out and establishing a free state. This political desire was joined with the religious hope of a Messiah who would deliver the people and reestablish the golden age of David. There were constant conflicts between various groups of Jews, all hoping for a better world. The Pharisees placed their hope in conformity to the Torah. A group called the Essenes were separatists. They demanded a withdrawal from the impurities of the secular world and various corrupt aspects of Jewish life. Finally, the Zealots were a group of political radicals who wanted the Romans driven out of Palestine so Israel could be restored to political power and prominence. All of these groups were looking for deliverance from a present which they believed could not get any worse.

The authorities had been cracking down on the more radical and vocal elements among the Jewish people. To be specific, John the Baptizer had been arrested. The Pharisees bitterly opposed this strange man with his message of repentance. John even went so far as to denounce Herod publicly as a sinner. Hence, John was arrested. Those in power felt secure and thought their problems ended. There would always be radical preachers who would excite the people's imagination. They could be tolerated within limits. Yet there was a point beyond which they could not go. To do so invited arrest and even death.

Just when those in power were breathing easy and the people were breathing their last, out of the wilderness came Jesus of Nazareth. This Jesus, son of Joseph and a carpenter; baptized by this crazy man, John; and lacking formal training came into Galilee "preaching the Gospel of God." And there was something and someone far greater than John and his baptism of water. This Jesus of Nazareth came preaching a baptism of fire which would transform the hearts of all who were opened to good news. Yet, as we know, not all receive good news as acceptable news. On this ordinary day, behold, God was doing a new thing!

Jesus: "The time is fulfilled, and the Kingdom of God is at hand; repent, and believe in the Gospel."

Benjamin (a Pharisee): "Teacher, this doctrine of yours is quite appealing. Perhaps you could expand a bit on it."

Jesus: "Why do I get the feeling that when you call me 'Teacher,' you do so in an insulting way? Besides, Benjamin, my preaching is not a doctrine nor is it a formal teaching which rests in the head but does not change the heart."

Samuel (an Essene): "Of course, this is not a doctrine or some teaching on the Torah which compromises what God wants. I know, Jesus, you are calling us to separate ourselves from the sinners. What you are giving us is a rigorous ethic by which to live. I greatly admire your 'getting tough with sin' approach."

Jesus: "You misunderstand who I am and what I am about even more than Benjamin. You speak about separating ourselves from the sinners. Just why do you think I have come? Just who do you think the sinners are?"

Samuel: "Help me to understand. Answer your own questions for me."

Jesus: "I have not come to condemn and cast into hell all who do not measure up to some standard you or someone else makes up. I have come to search for the lost and displaced. I have come to announce healing to those who hurt. I want to be found among those who are rejected and unaccepted. I am the physician who has come to heal those who are in pain. I want to tell everyone of the Father's un-

bounded love. All who repent will be accepted and
healed. Samuel, don't you see yourself in all this?
Don't you need healing?"

Samuel: "All that you have said strikes me as just another
compromise of what God wants. We have to return
to basics while there is still time. There is too
much . . ."

Jesus: "Too much good news, Samuel? Is the problem
that you can't handle the fact that God is generous
and loving and forgiving? Why does it scare you so
that God wants all his children to be with him? This
does not take anything away from you. In fact, the
banquet is enriched each time a child comes to his
or her senses and makes the journey homeward."

Nadab (a Zealot): "I find myself being frustrated with all three
of you. While each day the Romans inflict greater
humiliation and hardship on the people, all you
can do is talk. Benjamin, what relief has your
Torah brought? You, Samuel, you wait for some
magic deliverance. The sun has gotten to you. And
you, Jesus, you speak about the Kingdom, but you
don't seem to know what the Kingdom is about."

Jesus: "Oh, but I do, Nadab. Remember, there are two
very important words which follow 'Kingdom,'
namely, 'of God.' The Kingdom I was sent to
proclaim is not the kingdom of Nadab or Judas or
any of your party members. It is the Kingdom of
God which is at hand. In fact, God's Kingdom is
among you and within you. This is a force far
greater than Caesar's.

Nadab: "Where are the fighters and liberators of this Kingdom? Do you really believe that the Romans are
going to just leave because of your words? We need
action. We need to take up the sword!"

Jesus: "Are *you* being realistic? The real enemies of all
people are sin and death. These are enemies which
must be driven out. No sword is capable of such a

victory. It is only the Kingdom of God which can bring a true and lasting peace. This is not the illusion of peace promised by those who flash swords or fight fire with fire. True peace is God's gift. The world cannot give this peace or take it away."

Nadab: "How does one enlist in this Kingdom of God?"

Jesus: "You must be willing to let your heart be changed. Your whole being must undergo a radical transformation. Your security can no longer be in the sword, the Torah, or some moral code which teaches you to love those who are like you and hate all others."

Samuel: "Even though I find little to like about Benjamin, I must admire his zeal for the Law. He is committed to something. Even Nadab is willing to die for liberation. Jesus, you seem to offer us words and a dream of a better future. But there is no substance."

Jesus: "What I am offering you is frightening. It is easy to die by the sword. It is easy to live in the desert comforted by an air of moral superiority. Zeal for the Law too often comes at the expense of the Spirit which alone gives life. I am offering you something to *LIVE* for. The old securities and values must be transformed and surpassed. I am not offering you human certainty, but a blessed hope."

Benjamin: "When will this Kingdom of God be established? How will we know it is here? What are the signs of its presence?"

Jesus: "These are important questions. The Kingdom of God is at hand. It is at work among you this very moment. The danger is that you will miss it. You will be involved in many 'important' things but miss what is most crucial. Set your heart on God's Kingdom and all that you hoped for, and more, will be yours."

Nadab: "What are its signs? Where will the capital of this Kingdom be?"

Jesus: "The signs of the Kingdom are everywhere at work this very moment. The sinner is being called home to the Father. The outcasts are being welcomed at the Lord's table. The poor and forgotten are having the good news preached to them. The sick and hurting are being healed. God is ruling in the lives and hearts of the people. Can't you see it?"

Samuel: "What I see is a lack of respect for the Law. What I see are people who are chasing every radical who comes along promising deliverance. What I see is . . ."

Jesus: "What I see among each of you is a fearful story of God. Benjamin, your God wants people to give him a show of external conformity to a set of rules. Samuel, your God wants believers who are perfect and are afraid of being contaminated. And you, Nadab, your God wants followers who are brave enough to die. What I am offering you is a vision in which your God and Father wants you to be brave enough to live. God doesn't want your external offerings of conformity and moral self-righteousness. God wants your heart to be renewed and reborn. This calls for greater courage and spiritual maturity than anything you are demanding."

Samuel: "How so?"

Nadab: "Yes, how so? What is so courageous about your message?"

Jesus: "The courage to live within the vision of God's Kingdom is a courage which requires more than the willingness to face a sword or a code. You face God's radical claim on your lives. You must open your hearts to grace so that you can love the enemy, give generously to all in need, avoid judging, and be willing to forgive as you have been forgiven. And most of all . . ."

Benjamin:	"Most of all this seems to me to be just pious talk."
Jesus:	"Most of all, you must learn to be a person of joy."
Nadab:	"Joy? What does joy have to do with anything? Daily, the people are being driven into the ground and you speak about joy. There is no joy."
Jesus:	"Yes, Nadab, joy. This joy comes from being part of God's Kingdom which will not be overcome. God will triumph. The decisive battle is already underway. Not a battle of ideologies and armies, but a battle of the most profound dimensions. The very forces engaged in battle are those of good and evil. But, be assured, God will triumph. Joy comes from knowing sin and death have lost their ultimate power. The victory of the Kingdom is not one understood by earthly kings and soldiers. God's victory will not be stopped by Rome or even death. God's victory is that of love over hatred; hope over despair; life over death; and light over darkness. How can you help but not be filled with joy? You can't help but celebrate. The real question for each of you is simply this: are you strong enough to celebrate? Are you wise enough to be confident in God's victory? Are you trusting enough to hope that God really cares for you?"

We see in the above dialogue Jesus refusing to be domesticated or controlled by human categories or expectations. He cannot be labelled (or libeled) by any group which seeks their own ends above the Kingdom of God. Jesus transcended all the groups and controversies of his day. Jesus came with unique authority to announce the Kingdom of God. And this proclamation provides a transvaluation of all existing values. Perhaps what is most disconcerting about Jesus is his refusal to provide us with a blueprint for moral goodness, a just social order, and a religion which seeks control and power. Father Andrew Greeley, in his *The Jesus Myth*, writes:

Perhaps one of the reasons for the many controversies that have raged over Jesus of Nazareth is the difficulty in classifying him. For some, he seems a simple ethical preacher; to others, a mystical prophet; to others, an eschatological visionary; to yet others, a political revolutionary; and to still others, the founder of a church . . . He is a hard man to categorize. He does not seem to fit into any of our neat labels, and this problem of figuring out where exactly Jesus stands is not a new one. Even in his own time he puzzled most of his contemporaries . . . In other words, Jesus went about providing answers to questions that no one was asking and refusing to answer the questions everyone thought important. He resolutely refused to permit himself to be part of any of the principal religious or political currents of the environment in which he lived. One can imagine that a frequent question people asked about him was, "But where does he really stand?"

Jesus does not provide us with a hitching-post on which we can rest and let God do it all. Jesus does provide us with a sign-post which points us to the Kingdom of God as here and not yet. There are quite specific ways of acting: in addition to refraining from killing, we must not be overcome by anger; before we worship, we need to be reconciled with one another; not simply our physical acts but even our thoughts can make us impure; love is not simply for the one who is like us but for the enemy as well; our religious actions are worthy of God only if done with the right intention; seek treasures which cannot be placed in a bank but are hidden in the fields of our everyday lives; and avoid seeking our rights when injured but rather act with a generosity that moves us to turn the other cheek, give our cloak as well as our coat, and when someone forces us to go one mile, go with him two miles.

As we read the list above, we are moved to ask, "Is Jesus really serious?" The answer is yes — Jesus is joyfully serious. This answer, however, only makes sense within the vision of God's Kingdom. Apart from the guiding vision of the Kingdom

of God, all that Jesus asks of us is absurd. To misquote the
words of G. K. Chesterton: Christianity has not been tried and
found wanting but it has been tried and found too difficult. We
would fare much better if Jesus had laid out for us a specific set
of actions and requirements. We then could have creatively
used our intellect to find the loopholes. We could have lived
minimally by simply doing what is required — but no more.
We could stand before Jesus and demand our just reward for
following the rules. Salvation would be something we had
earned. The ministry and Paschal mystery of Jesus would be
useless. Jesus would be reduced to simply another great
prophet or teacher. We could apply his teachings and save
ourselves.

Jesus, however, provides us with a vision of the Kingdom
of God and invites us to tell our personal stories through this
vision. Who can do this? By ourselves, we are helpless. But we
are not left to our own designs. We can risk being disciples of
Jesus and live as citizens of the kingdom of God. Why? What
gives us the blessed hope and power to trust that the Really
Real is gracious and loving and caring? Jesus invites us to
learn from the simple signs of graciousness which abound:

> Look at the birds of the air: they neither sow nor reap nor
> gather into barns, and yet your heavenly Father feeds
> them. Are you not of more value than they? . . . Consider
> the lilies of the field, how they grow; they neither toil nor
> spin; yet I tell you, even Solomon in all his glory was not
> arrayed like one of these. But if God so clothes the grass
> of the field, which today is alive and tomorrow is thrown
> into the oven, will he not much more clothe you, O men of
> little faith? But seek first his kingdom and his righteous-
> ness, and all shall be yours as well. (Mk 6:25-33)

The words of Jesus are foolishness to the worldly-wise.
His vision is a nightmare to those who desire power and glory.
His invitation is absurd to those who counsel prudence and
playing it safe. This vision of Jesus is simply too good to be
true. Things are simply not that way. He can't be serious. But

what if things really are this way? What if Jesus is joyfully serious? What if things really are this good and gracious and caring? What if, indeed.

The Necessity of Community

The vision which Jesus offers of the Kingdom requires a community. Without community, we tell our own highly privatized stories apart from the story of Jesus and the Kingdom. The Christian community is a living, ongoing reality of all — past, present, and yet to be — who share the story or stories of Jesus. The Christian community is that body of believers who remain in the world, throughout history, keeping "the dangerous memory" of Jesus alive. The Christian community shares the story of what Yahweh has done for his creation and the various signs of his Lordship in history. The Christian community keeps telling and retelling what Yahweh has done in Jesus. The story of Yahweh at work in Jesus is one of victory and hope. In the face of death, life is stronger. When darkness abounds, yet light abides. When sin is at its greatest power, God's grace is greater still. When all hope is lost, the invitation to trust is extended with greater intensity. Down through the centuries, Christians have gathered to hear these stories and enact them in the Eucharist.

In our highly rational world of clear and distinct ideas, the notion of a Christian story or narrative may seem childish, unsophisticated, or even disrespectful. A brief, but important, word about story needs to be said. Biblical scholar Luke T. Johnson indicates that one of the primary tasks of the theologian is helping the community of faith to tell and tell again its story(ies). Unfortunately, this storytelling ministry is often trivialized as not befitting the professional theologian. Professor Johnson writes:

> If we only appreciate storytelling as a pleasant diversion, we will not grasp the importance of this function. The

study of societies — primitive and complex alike — shows us that although some forms of storytelling do serve a recreational purpose, others perform a more fundamental *re-creational* role within the life of communities, shaping both the group and its understanding of reality. This kind of storytelling has to do with personal and group identity. The story of my life — if I can tell it — reveals who I am. Our communal story — if we can give it shape — tells others, and first of all ourselves, how we have come to be what we are. In the life of groups we find such storytelling in the myths of origin and those which accompany rites of passage. In the life of individuals, such personal storytelling is found in confession or therapy, where the telling of the whole story not only expresses a stage of intimacy and trust but also reveals at once to the other and to the self who one is. (*Decision Making in the Church*)

The importance of story is not limited to secular groups but touches the very core of the religious community. Stories form the *living tradition* around which the community of faith learns to speak the language of faith; to practice the gestures which indicate that the story is not just a head game; and to acquire the vision of faith necessary to see God at work here and now. All of these elements are present in the community which centers its life in the self-revelation of God. At the most fundamental level of the religious community's life is this belief: God can be encountered and known in history. The stories we tell are our reminders that our faithful struggle is never completed by any one generation but continues until Christ comes again in glory. And until he comes, we tell of his wonders in countless stories. Jesuit theologian Father Tad Dunne, S.J., in his study on Bernard Lonergan, S.J., devotes a chapter to storytelling. Father Dunne sees the ongoing activity of storytelling as our way of being drawn into Mystery.

The know-it-alls among us are impatient with good stories because they prefer certitude to mysteries. They hope to

slice some moral from the heart of a story or enshrine
some pithy line on a poster. But such categorical reduc-
tions of good stories can never exhaust their meaning . . .
no single event or set of events, nor any of their stories
can ever exhaust the total potentiality of complete intel-
ligibility, existence, or goodness . . . good stories are
more than we can handle, and yet they fail to slake our
thirst for Mystery. Good stories, like good liturgies, span
the chasm between divine Mystery and human reckon-
ing. (*Lonergan and Spirituality*)

The Christian goes even further when it comes to
Mystery. This Mystery has become visible in the Person of
Jesus. This visible Mystery has become our poor flesh inviting
us to be disciples of the Kingdom of God. Jesus calls us to tell
our personal stories *within* the horizon of the Kingdom. In no
way is our individuality destroyed. Rather, within the Kingdom, we become who we were always meant to be — mature
children of our loving Father. It is from our community of faith,
with its stories of Jesus, that we learn to see God and ourselves
aright.
　　What does it mean to see God and ourselves in the right
way? Stanley Hauerwas has made a sustained and creative use
of the categories: narrative, community, vision, and virtue.
Drawing on his brilliant analysis, we can offer the following: to
see God and ourselves in the proper perspective means that we
experience our lives and all creation as a gift from a gracious
and loving God. Our fundamental stance toward reality should
be one of openness and gratitude. Such an openness bespeaks
a willingness to receive all that God has *already given in Jesus
and the abiding Spirit*. With the recognition of our giftedness
comes one of the deepest of religious emotions — gratitude.
We give thanks all our days to the Lord who has gifted all our
days. To see the world, self, and God aright means that we
understand ourselves to be creatures in the hands of a loving
Creator. The world and all therein belongs to God and is
entrusted to us so that we might share in God's very work of

creation and care. Such a vision runs counter to our worldly wisdom and the pervading vision of man-as-will-to-power.

The Christian vision articulates a story of realism when it comes to seeing things as they are. Namely, the world and the human heart exist in estrangement from God. There is a general and pervading spirit of rebellion against the sovereign rule of God. This is sin — the refusal to see God's world *as* God's world and to assert our own will in opposition to the loving will of God. We live *as if* we are in control of our ultimate destiny and the meaning of history. This vision of man-in-control ruptures the fundamental unity of reality which God seeks to establish by persuasive love rather than by coercive force. Stanley Hauerwas writes:

> The Christian story trains us to see that in most of our life we act as if this is not God's world and therein lies our fundamental sin . . . we distort our own and the world's nature. Therefore sin implies not just a claim about human behavior but a claim about the way things are . . . sin is the positive attempt to overreach our power as creatures . . . its fundamental form is self-deception . . . our sin — our fundamental sin — is the assumption that we are the creators of history through which we acquire and possess our character. Sin is the form our character takes as a result of our fear that we will be "nobody" if we lose control of our lives.
>
> Moreover our need to be in control is the basis for the violence of our lives. For since our "control" and "power" cannot help but be built on an insufficient basis, we must use force to maintain the illusion that we are in control. We are deeply afraid of losing what unity of self we have achieved. Any idea or person threatening that unity must be either manipulated or eliminated. We fear others because they always stand as an implicit challenge to our deceptions. Thus it seems the inherent necessity of all people to have or create an enemy.
>
> (*The Peaceable Kingdom*)

The need to tell our personal story within the Christian story(ies); the ability to see the world with the vision of Jesus and the Kingdom; and to know that our existence is a gift from a gracious God is anything but abstract theology, Platonic ideas, or unsophisticated piety unworthy of believers come of age. The Christian life is just that — the daily dying and rising in union with Jesus within the "peaceable Kingdom." We daily pick up our cross and deny those thousand and one impulses to self-glory, self-assertion, pride, hatred, violence, and the egoism which says that we are in control. We respond to those "finer angels" within which move us to search for truth; to live lives of quiet, uncelebrated heroism; to speak out on behalf of those who are ignored and rejected; to commit ourselves to our daily duties simply because it is our duty; to remain faithful to the smallest, deep-down things which enhance the lives of others; and to follow our conscience and keep our promises when hard-headed practicality counsels otherwise. Not only on starry nights and days of cool breezes but in the seemingly ordinary aspects of life, we lift our hearts and sing, "How great thou art!" Again, Professor Hauerwas:

> The Christian life is a constant struggle to wrestle the truth out of the everyday. Recent Christian ethics has concentrated its attention on the crisis situation or the "big event." The Christian life is defined in relation not to the humdrum but to revolution and conflict; the everyday is morally uninteresting. But when the Christian life is understood as the life of attention, the emphasis is placed squarely on the everyday. For the moral significance of our lives is not constituted by moving from one significant social problem to another; rather it depends upon our willingness to work at being human through the manifold particularity of our lives. It is a matter not of finding the ultimate truth but of finding what the truth is in the small questions that confront us every day. It is a matter of what we do with our time, whether we are willing to work to make our marriages worthwhile, how well we perform our

everyday tasks. The main problem of the moral life is not to come to monumental decisions but to live through the contingencies of our lives. (*Vision and Virtue*)

The Christian story and vision are learned within the community of faith. Such learning is a process that extends over the whole of one's life. The call to repent and reform one's life is present at the beginning of Jesus' preaching about the Kingdom and endures until we see him face to face. To be a disciple of Jesus is to place one's whole life under the claims of the Kingdom and to freely accept the cost of conversion. It is to this process of conversion that we now turn our attention.

Conversion: A Theo-Philosophical Note

In recent times, a significant body of work has been left to us by the noted Jesuit philosopher and theologian, Bernard Lonergan, S.J., concerning the experience of conversion; or better yet — conversions. I am indebted throughout this brief discussion to Fathers Edward K. Braxton, Charles E. Curran, and Tad Dunne, S.J. Naturally, Father Lonergan's work deserves to be read on its own. However, these theologians have helped us to gain immense insight into the profound thought of Lonergan and have extended his vision in exciting new ways. A good deal of Father Lonergan's work is contained in various articles. However, the topic of conversion is discussed in his significant work, *Insight: A Study of Human Understanding*.

Upon hearing the word "conversion," we tend to think of a dramatic breakthrough in which one becomes "a new being." Two of the more familiar examples would be the conversion of the Apostle Paul and St. Augustine. Few of us are blessed (or burdened) with such profound displays of amazing grace. For most of us, it is the daily challenge to pick up our cross and follow Jesus. There are few, if any, dramatic moments when it becomes clear. Often, we are not able to mark the day and the hour when "amazing grace saved a wretch like me." Father

Edward K. Braxton has written a most helpful book (*The Wisdom Community*) for those who desire to apply the work of Lonergan to various levels of Church life (parish, university, and theological). On the topic of conversion, Father Braxton writes:

> The word "conversion," however, is somewhat problematic. Many Roman Catholics think of it as an experience available only to Christians of other traditions or those who have no religious affiliation and wish to become Catholics. While this may rightly be called conversion, conversion as it is intended here is available to, and needed by, Catholics as much as anyone else. In some Protestant communions conversion means the acceptance of Christ as one's personal savior in a highly dramatic and emotional style as with some "born again" Christians. For still others, conversion may mean a kind of Gnostic election that puts one on a new spiritual plane as with some forms of Charismatic and Pentecostal experiences. (*The Wisdom Community*)

Father Charles E. Curran, in his discussion on Lonergan and conversion, offers the following as additional reasons for the Catholic community's uneasiness and neglect of conversion as a theological topic:

- the concept of conversion denotes change, interiority, and a personal encounter with Jesus. Traditional Catholic theology is more at home with the classicist approach to theology (static, substance, community, and the eternal). Father Curran quotes Lonergan on the topic of conversion: "It is a topic little studied in traditional theology since there remains very little of it when one reaches the universal, the abstract and the static." (Quotation taken from: Lonergan, *Theology of Renewal*, vol. I, 44.)
- the concept of conversion has traditionally been limited to a non-Catholic becoming a Catholic. Conversion was understood as "joining the Church." The concept of

conversion was usually discussed within dogmatic theology under the influence of scholastic philosophical language.

- the concept of conversion has been neglected by Catholic moral theology. The approach of traditional Catholic moral theology manuals tended to emphasize moral actions in isolation from the human person. Moral theology stressed the outward actions in terms of accepted norms rather than the process of an inward change of heart.

- the concept of conversion was neglected due to a too individualistic view of sin. Sin was understood as an individual act which violated a moral norm or objective law. The social dimensions of sin were also neglected. Sin was confined to the heart and one's personal behavior. At times, recent Catholic statements and encyclicals failed to take seriously the reality and power of human sinfulness. (See, for example, the optimistic encyclical by Pope John XXIII, *Pacem in Terris*)

- finally, as previously mentioned by Father Braxton, the concept of conversion has struck the Catholic mind as "too Protestant."

(See also the excellent discussion on Lonergan and conversion by Father Charles E. Curran, "Dialogue with Bernard Lonergan: The Concept of Conversion," in his book, *Catholic Moral Theology in Dialogue*)

The discussion of conversion in the writings of Bernard Lonergan provides the Catholic community with an excellent resource for appreciating this most fundamental of Christian experiences. Also, Lonergan's discussion fits well within the framework of our previous presentations on story, vision, and community. We need to ask: what does Lonergan mean by conversion?

Lonergan holds that each person lives within a horizon or field of vision through which he or she relates to the world. Our horizon forms our world view and structures the way we encounter, interpret, and value the world. There are many ways in which we encounter reality: biologically (awareness of our bodily condition in its various needs, impulses, and drives); psychologically (awareness of our inner world with its various morals and feelings and desires); mystically (an encounter with the supernatural which cannot be named but is known to be real — Really Real); socially (this is our world-with-others in ever greater forms of complexity and interactive connectedness); aesthetically (an awareness of beauty as the harmony of harmonies); dramatically (the expression of our unique story, but through which we belong to something larger than ourselves); and intellectually (the drive of the mind to know not merely facts of information but the underlying Truth and Wisdom of the whole of reality). It is at this last level or structure of human experience, the intellectual, that the question of God is raised. We seek self-transcendence and we desire to know in an ultimate way. The heart's deepest longing of the human person as human is for God. To leave this longing unfulfilled is to deny an essential aspect of our being. Father Lonergan writes:

> The question of God, then, lies within man's horizon. Man's transcendent subjectivity is mutilated or abolished, unless he is stretching forth towards the intelligible, the unconditioned, the good of value. The reach, not of his attainment, but of his intending is unrestricted. There lies within his horizon a region for the divine, a shrine for ultimate holiness. It cannot be ignored. The atheist may pronounce it empty. The agnostic may urge that he find his investigation has been inconclusive. The contemporary humanist will refuse to allow the question to arise. But their negations presuppose the spark in our cloud, our native orientation to the divine.
>
> (*Method in Theology*)

The process of conversion, then, is one in which we experience a change in our horizon. This process of conversion is a radical transformation which extends throughout the various ways (patterns) in which we experience reality. There is a

profound movement throughout the various realms of experience (biological, psychological, etc.) so that we come to
spiritual integration. We move towards a wholeness in our
ways of experiencing reality. We come to know that God's love
is at work in us healing the divisions of our being. Father Tad
Dunne, S.J. writes the following on the process of spiritual
integration:

> It is the capacity to move through these realms of meaning
> intelligently. That is, the kind of authenticity needed
> today is the kind by which a person has a basic under-
> standing of these different realms of meaning and can
> move from one to another as the situation demands . . .
> spiritual integration allows a person to ground all the
> workings of the mind and all the practical decisions of a
> responsible life in the love of divine Mystery . . . So
> spiritual integration is primarily a commitment to using
> one's head and heart not only about the realities of the
> outer world, but particularly about the head and heart
> themselves. It is a habit of soul, not a body of knowledge.
> (*Lonergan and Spirituality*)

Lonergan holds that we can experience a number of forms
of conversion: religious, theistic, Christian, ecclesial, moral,
and intellectual. All these forms of conversion are crucial and
interrelated. The experience of wonder, awe, or limit gives rise
to the questions of the sacred or holy. This religious conversion
is made explicit, or named, in the theistic conversion. We call
the source of our wonder God. Christian conversion is the
belief that God has encountered us uniquely in the person of
Jesus who is truly God and truly human. The belief in Jesus as
the Son of God moves us into a community which shares the
same story(ies) about who Jesus is and what he means for us
and our salvation. However, belief must be put into practice
and guide our actions. Moral conversion is a lifelong process of
living the Paschal Mystery. Finally, we come to the process of
intellectual conversion by which we group in varying degrees
the interrelatedness of all reality. We come to understand and

experience truth as one. We look beyond the seeming fragmentation of experience and see a wholeness and integration. Intellectual conversion is the process of reflection and integration.

Admittedly, all this may seem very abstract and "too philosophical"; however, if we connect Lonergan's understanding of conversion with our previous discussion concerning story, community, and vision, we can offer the following: conversion is that process which extends over the whole of our lives by which we come to expand our horizon or world view in such a way that the story of God in Jesus becomes the focal point of our horizon or story. We are able to say with the Apostle Paul: for me, life means Christ. And again, it is no longer *I* who lives (*I* being the self-centered ego) but Christ who lives in *me* (the *me* is that self enlivened by the story of Jesus). In order for this process of conversion (the telling our story in terms of the Jesus-story) to begin and to be sustained, we place ourselves within the community of faith which enacts this story of Jesus Christ. Our conversion is within and supported by the community and is perfected by the grace of the Holy Spirit. Finally, our conversion extends beyond beliefs to actions. We enact the story of Jesus by acknowledging our lives as loving gifts from God. We love in imitation of Jesus. We really open ourselves to Jesus so as to daily "put on Christ."

Perhaps this may seem too general; lacking in details; and not providing us with specifics as to what to do in a given situation. The notion of moral conversion may seem too subjective. The door is open to doing our own thing. This notion of conversion can strike us as easy at first blush. Yet on closer inspection, we see how much is being required of us and how profound the change required. Christian, moral, and intellectual conversion is the radical call and acceptance of discipleship. In 'fear and trembling,' we place our very being in the care of God. We pick up our cross daily and follow Jesus on the road to Jerusalem. The temptation is always present to proclaim Jesus as the Messiah and, at the same time, steer clear of Golgotha. We must continually live with those harsh

but essential words of Jesus: "Get behind me, Satan, for you
are speaking the words of man and not of God." This costly
grace of conversion provides the horizon in which Jesus Christ
becomes all in all as well as our personal all. Conversion and
the costly grace of discipleship form the horizon through which
the concrete moral problems are understood. Concerning such
a horizon, moral theologian Enda McDonagh writes:

> Discipleship or the following of Jesus Christ provides one
> key description of moral life for Christians which has at
> least a secure basis in the New Testament. Its value as an
> inspiring vision depends on the faith commitment and
> scriptural awareness of the believer. Its potential for
> resolving difficulties in concrete situations is more prob-
> lematic. Yet one's basic commitment and overall vision
> provide the context for all authentic solutions to moral
> problems and the following of Christ may give more
> precise indications in actual situations than one's reluc-
> tance for moral effort may admit. (*Doing the Truth*)

Hence we can say that as we confront the small and large
moral problems of daily Christian living, we need not be
anxious about what we are to say or do; for this will be given us
in that hour; "for it is not we who speak, but the Spirit of our
Father speaking through us" (Mt 10:19-20).

Conversion, Virtue, and the Pastorals

The experience of conversion is nothing new to the pages
of the Scriptures. These stories of conversion span the range
from the highly dramatic to the slow process of turning to God.
Conversion need not be a turning from sin to grace. It can be
the dramatic encounter of the human person with God. This
dramatic encounter takes the form of leaving the old securities,
identities, values, and beliefs and becoming a new person.
One dies to the old self and follows the invitation of God to
begin anew. The examples of Abraham in the Hebrew Bible

and the call of the disciples by Jesus in the Christian
Scriptures are but two of the more familiar examples. No
discussion of conversion would be satisfactory without including the highly dramatic conversion of the Apostle Paul. This
zealous Jew encountered the Lord Jesus on the road to
Damascus. Life was never the same. Writing to his beloved
Philippians, Paul gave the following testimony:

> But whatever gain I had, I counted as loss for the sake of
> Christ. Indeed I count everything as loss because of the
> surpassing worth of knowing Christ Jesus as my Lord. For
> his sake I have suffered the loss of all things, and count
> them as refuse, in order that I may gain Christ, and be
> found in him, not having a righteousness of my own,
> based on law, but that which is through faith in Christ,
> the righteousness from God that depends on faith; that I
> may know him and the power of his resurrection, and may
> share his sufferings, becoming like him in his death, that
> if possible I may attain the resurrection from the dead.
> (Ph 3:7-11)

The story of Paul's conversion played a prominent role
throughout his ministry, and was especially important for his
two young associates — Timothy and Titus. After being apart
for some time, the three ministers of the Gospel found time to
share a meal and some of their recent experiences. But the
interest in Paul's conversion was a constant in their many
conversations. This evening's gathering is no different.
Timothy raises the issue of conversion.

Timothy: "Paul, tell us once again about being knocked from
             your horse on the road to Damascus. I really envy
             you that experience. After all, there can be little
             doubt as to what the Lord wanted of you."

Paul: "Once again, Timothy, I was walking, not riding,
             on the way to Damascus. I think my horse belongs
             next to the Garden of Eden apple. If we depended
             on that horse, we wouldn't ride and if we required
             that apple, we'd starve!"

Titus:	"I didn't realize that you were given to demythologization."
Paul:	"Neither did I. In fact, I am not sure I can even say the word! But I do want to say something about my conversion in a serious way. Remember that immediately following my experience I couldn't see, eat or drink for three days. It was as if I had died. In a profound sense, I had. My old supports and certainties no longer guided my journey nor nourished my spirit. I was rendered totally needy. I have come to see how necessary this was so that I would boast only about what the Lord has done for me and through me."
Timothy:	"But don't forget, Paul, you were spared the uncertainty that troubles so many of us. You had no doubts that this was Jesus and this is what he wanted of you."
Paul:	"I only wish it were true. My experience on the way to Damascus was not an exemption from the human condition. In fact, during my trials and periods in prison, I experienced my share of depression and doubts. Thoughts rushed through my head that I had made a wrong turn, so to speak. How could this Lord of mine let his servant experience such things? The jails, the shipwrecks, the lean years, and the heated debates have been anything but easy."
Timothy:	"But you must admit that there is little of this human drama in your letters. You seem always to be strong."
Paul:	"I am only strong at the broken places. It is at the broken places that God's grace reaches perfection in us. Without an awareness of our weakness, we get the idea that we are in control. We come to believe that we are the masters of our own fate. This is spiritually tragic. The Lord has blessed me with thorns in the flesh, but also with wonderful

communities of support and healing. Even in the darkest times, I knew the Philippians were always praying for me. Even those Corinthians could be counted on in a tight spot. I have tried to share my journey through weakness to strength in terms of what the Lord has done for me."

Titus: "Are you saying that the conversion experience on the way to Damascus is a continuing experience?"

Paul: "Absolutely. Unfortunately, some believe all you need do is say, 'Jesus is Lord' and that's it. What that is is presumption and spiritual sloth. Some have come to even teach that all laws and doctrines can be done away with simply because one claims to have the Spirit. You know how some in the various communities have gone around teaching that the Lord has already returned. What damage they have done!"

Titus: "I know what you mean, Paul. Yet how does one know or judge the claims of another concerning conversion and the Spirit?"

Paul: "That's never easy. We must watch the way they live. Look to the fruits their lives produce. Remember, it is not we who have the Spirit, but the Spirit who grasps our inner being."

Titus: "What are these fruits of the Spirit?"

Paul: "I am sure you are familiar with my letter to the Colossians, since you read everything I write."

Titus: "Paul, I even read some of the things you *don't* write! Just kidding."

Paul: "If there were such a thing as an Irishman, you would be one! Anyway, the fruits of the Spirit are what some call virtue. We are to avoid fornication, impurity, passion, evil desire, and covetousness. We must rid ourselves of anger, wrath, malice, slander, and foul talk. We must not lie to one another."

Titus: "But that's all so negative."

Paul: "The negative has its place in moral training. But, of course, it is not the whole of moral conversion. We must become a new creature. We must practice compassion, kindness, lowliness, meekness, and patience. Just as the Lord has forgiven us, so must we learn to forgive one another. The perfection of all the virtues is love. As I have written to the Corinthians, the greatest of gifts is love. Without love, our gifts become possessions and sources of our vain boasting. Without love, our virtues become splendid vices."

Timothy: "The practice of the virtues is not just for those to whom we preach. We as ministers need to be men of virtue."

Paul: "That is well said, Timothy. In fact, it is crucial for you and Titus to aim at righteousness, godliness, faith, love, and gentleness. Above all, you must practice the virtue of steadfastness. You must hold firm to solid teaching and demand that the truth about Jesus be preached at all times. It is not so much the threat of physical abuse or the danger of playing fast and loose with sound teaching. There must be a constancy about our teaching and the way we live our teaching. Without such a development of character, a daily and sustained conversion, we will not be able to fight the good fight of faith."

Recent moral philosophy and theological ethics have experienced a renewed interest in the study of virtue. Many, both within and outside the modern academy, have voiced their growing dissatisfaction with much of contemporary ethical reflection, which seems divorced from the concerns of everyday life. Such ethical analysis seems to be the special domain of the expert with little regard for the moral development (character) of the person. There seems to many to be an overemphasis on behavior without considering the *kind* of person one is and is becoming. Moral philosopher Gilbert C. Meilaender, in his brilliant book, *The Theory and Practice of Virtue*, writes:

> This return to an ethic of virtue suggests a widespread dissatisfaction with an understanding of the moral life which focuses primarily on duties, obligations, troubling moral dilemmas, and borderline cases. Such cases are interesting, and certainly important when they arise, but we must admit that many of us go through long stretches of life in which we do not have to decide whether to frame one innocent man in order to save five, whether to lie to the secret police in order to hide someone, whether to approve aborting the ninth, possibly retarded, child of a woman whose husband has deserted her, and so forth. An ethic of virtue seeks to focus not only on such moments of great anxiety and uncertainty in life but also on the continuities, the habits of behavior which make us the persons we are.

The attractiveness of the ethic of virtue is not only motivated by an appeal to everyday experience, but by an appeal to a long and distinguished history of moral discourse within both the Christian and Western traditions. In the words of Stanley Hauerwas: "For the Greeks, as well as the Christians, virtue was the central concept for moral reflection . . . morality began with descriptions of the virtuous life. Ethics grew from questions of what individuals should be; armed with answers, the ancients then turned to prescriptive modes" (*A Community of Character*). These words of Professor Hauerwas are both accurate and troubling, for there is a danger in our return to the ethic of virtue.

The ethic of virtue can be seen, wrongly, as a set of practices which arms us with answers. This is most attractive in a world of uncertainty and moral confusion. The ethic of virtue is viewed as a means to calm our moral anxiety and keep others in line. We know what is expected of us and others. We are able to clearly judge the good and the bad. Also disquieting

is the idea that virtues are what *we* practice on the way to
self-perfection. The Christian story has always been aware of
such a danger. We can come to view virtues as possessions
which we earn. Christian theology rejects this view as boastful
and proud. Again, the words of Professor Hauerwas deserve
attention:

> Augustine argued that in a significant sense virtue cannot
> be a possession of the soul. On the contrary, as a gift of
> God "either virtue exists beyond the soul, or if we are not
> allowed to give the name of virtue except to the habit and
> disposition of the wise soul, which can exist only in the
> soul, we must allow that the soul follows after something
> else in order that virtue may be produced in itself."
> Unless this "something else" is God, the virtues are but
> forms of self-love and become nothing more than glorious
> vices. (*A Community of Character*)

Without the recognition that all is from God, we easily
become prideful and intolerant of others. Our virtues become
splendid vices if we fail to put on love which opens our eyes to
that "Tremendous Lover." Self-mastery can easily become
self-righteousness. The virtues become ends in themselves
rather than means to the God who has blessed us with all
things. Professor Meilaender cautions that the ethic of virtue
runs the risk of being one more manifestation of our narcis-
sistic age. In effect, we take up moral jogging and eat the
health food of virtue so as to whip our character into shape. It is
not the body beautiful but the character in control that we come
to prize and promote and envy. Professor Meilaender quotes
Waldo Beach and H. Richard Niebuhr with approval:

> The monastery was to be a lifelong "school of the Lord's
> service," where strict discipline and exactly prescribed
> routines lead to the "commencement" of spiritual perfec-
> tion. But in the curriculum of salvation the monk could
> easily become more concerned with his relation to the
> discipline than to the end for which the discipline was

set, or, to speak by analogy, more concerned about getting grades than wisdom . . . He was encouraged to try to outdo his fellow monks in humility; hence he might look down on those whom he had surpassed. Thus the deadly sin of pride, in the guise of its opposite, forever shadowed the monk as he struggled to achieve humility, a shadow inevitable in an ethics that conceives blessedness as something achieved by the self-conscious self.

(*Christian Ethics: Sources of the Living Tradition*)

The Apostle Paul knew well the dangers of a blessedness achieved by the self-conscious self. Conversion, the turning over of one's whole being to the Lord, is a grace which we do not earn but can only gratefully receive. It is not something that is owed us, but a gift which is offered. It is love, the greatest of divine gifts, which reminds us of how much we have received and how much we can share. For in the end, all is gift and all comes from the God who is Love. Professor Meilaender ends his book on virtue with these profound words about grace:

This is the mystery of grace, of a gift which demands and requires nothing in return, not even gratitude. This gift of God is really a gift, perhaps the only real gift ever given. It is not cheap, but it is free. It cannot be cheap; for its price is, as Luther says in his explanation of the second article of the creed, "the holy precious blood and innocent suffering and death" of the Son of the Father. But it is really free — the gift of which even our best gifts are but halting imitations. Which is why one of the ancient prayers of the Church begins: "O God, you declare your almighty power *chiefly* in showing mercy and pity." This God, the Father of this Son, is the One who now says to us: freely you have received, freely give.

(*The Theory and Practice of Virtue*)

Concluding Word

Our reflections began with the dialogue between Jane and Helen. The end of their conversation was both typical and unsatisfactory. Typical, in that we often find ourselves stalled in moral traffic when it comes to moral discourse. We simply find ourselves in a state of agreeing to disagree even, and most troubling, about the most fundamental of beliefs. Unsatisfactory, in that we feel we should be able to provide clear, distinct, and compelling reasons as to why we believe as we do. The other person is often unmoved by our explanations. Frustration knows no bounds. What might Helen have said to Jane in light of our discussions?

Before we offer a critique of a person's actions, we need to address the more basic issues of character, community, narrative, and virtue. As Christians, we have been schooled to see our lives as a gift from our loving God. This gift of our life is not given and then taken back, nor is it given by God who then forgets all about us. The gift of our lives is truly a gift to us by the God who remains faithful and loving throughout. God's gift of life is an everlasting commitment to us. This commitment is enduring, caring, respectful, free, and hopeful. God does not go back on his word. God's loving covenant is not dependent on the weakness and fickleness of the human heart.

It is around this fundamental belief, that life is a gift from our loving God, that we form a community which tells this story over and over. In sharing this story, we come to conforming loving, free obedience of our lives to this narrative. We desire our lives and relationships to be faithful, committed, caring, respectful, loving, and hopeful. We learn the gestures and virtues which help form the kind of character which indicates that God's story is our own. This is a constant process of conversion. Each day brings the daily struggle and joy of growing in the full stature of the people of God. Professor Stanley Hauerwas writes:

> . . . moral behavior involves more than simply the decisions and choices men make about specific problems; it also includes the kind of men they are (their character and virtues), the kind of beliefs they hold, and the way that they integrate and organize their resources and ener-

gies to form a coherent life plan. The moral life is not simply a matter of decision governed by publicly defensible principles and rules; we can only act in the world we see, a seeing partially determined by the kinds of beings we have become through the stories we have learned and embodied in our life plan. (*Vision and Virtue*)

To be specific, we as Christians do not engage in premarital and extramarital sexual behavior because of the kind of persons we are, formed through the stories of God we continually tell one another. The Christian story understands the marital relationship and human sexuality to be a special reflection of God's mysterious love for us. When we give ourselves in sexual love and join together in marriage, we are expressing and remembering the Lord until he comes again. To engage in sexual acts outside of the context of marriage is to tell a different story than the living narrative of the faith community. As Catholic Christians, we simply do not do such things because such actions and relationships are of a different narrative. Not only is premarital and extramarital sex of a different narrative, but we hold it to be a *wrong* narrative. The love of husband and wife is a mirror of the love between Christ and the Church. Such a love is faithful, sacrificial, life-giving, joyful, and committed over a lifetime. To engage in premarital and extramarital sex is not simply a matter of a different preference or an alternative lifestyle. Such actions and relationships are contrary to a major theme in our faith narrative. When we engage in such behavior, we tell a lie in the language of love. We profess one story with our words, but we live a quite different story with our actions. In the final analysis, it is the story we live with our lives which is true; all the rest is fiction.

At the end of all this, will Jane revise her beliefs and see the light? I would hope so, but there are no guarantees. All we can do, and this is quite a lot, is to continually be faithful to the story of our faith community. We must be constant in our commitment to God's truth in Jesus. We must preach the Word in and out of season. We must fight the good fight of faith and live morally honorable lives. Even as we are being poured out for the Gospel, we are at the same time being filled with the joy of the Spirit. None of our teaching, preaching, or witnessing is done out of a sense of moral or spiritual superiority. We tell and live the truth of our narrative in love. There is always a gap between our story and the stories of God. Our telling is always informed with the realism of our all too human condition. We find ourselves in the back of the church, asking for forgiveness. We are very much like the rest of humankind. We are in need of amazing grace which helps us to see how far we fall short of God's glory and, at the same time, how far God's love reaches. We are sinners in the hand and heart of a loving God. At the center of the moral life is the story of grace upon grace. The closing word, which is an invitation to *continue* the story, belongs to Professor Meilaender:

> Moral understanding and action depend on vision; vision depends on character; character must be shaped by those who come before us. But what justifies their claim to a version of moral truth? By whom was their character shaped? Aristotle must find a good lawgiver, Plato a philosopher-king, Kohlberg a moral expert. We do not, I think, produce such people naturally. We can transmit only the corrupt human stock, with its distorted vision, which is ours. Our need therefore exceeds our powers. What moral education requires is a revelation by which we can test our vision and a grace powerful enough to transform our character. Good ethics, it turns out, will require not just good politics but good theology.
>
> *(The Theory and Practice of Virtue)*

V

PASTORAL PRIEST:
Across the Generations

Throughout our discussions, the word "mystery" has been prominent. It was early admitted that this word was not to be counted as one of our contemporary "buzz words." The word "mystery" is often associated in the popular mind with superstition, science fiction (a strange blending of words!), and the failed attempt by those in religion to remain in control of a world which has come of age. In the popular mind, the word "mystery" is most unpopular. Hence, how are we to understand the priesthood? Like human existence, Church, ministry, teaching, and the moral life, the priesthood is intimately associated with mystery.

Father James A. Fischer, in his thoughtful book, *Priests: Images, Ideals, and Changing Roles*, writes:

> The essential battle is between secularism and spiritual values. Secularism means that we think we live in a self-contained universe that can be explained, controlled and provided for if only we have a little more research and a little more push. Spiritual values mean that there are realities beyond scientific investigation and control. Although doctors can prolong life, they are essentially losers. Only the spiritual person can survive sickness and death. That is what priests need to remind people of. That is what they need to interpret in the endless flow of secular living. Priests are mystery men.

While priests are proclaiming "the other dimension" of reality, they must always do so in light of daily life on earth. It is in the very marrow of daily existence that God's saving, amazing grace comes to us. There is nothing more mysterious than the ordinary and the everyday. Good liturgy, incarnate preaching, and believable teaching result from seeing, hearing, and feeling the "God who is beyond at work in our midst." Alan W. Watt, in his beautiful book, *Behold the Spirit*, wrote:

> God is the most obvious thing in the world . . . He is absolutely self-evident — the simplest, clearest and closest reality of life and consciousness. We are only unaware of Him because we are too complicated, for our vision is darkened by the complexity of pride. We seek beyond the horizon with our noses lifted high in the air, and fail to see that He lies at our very feet . . . We are like birds flying in quest of air, or men with lighted candles searching through the darkness for fire.

The priest as a man of mystery is called to help people see what is most obvious, present, and near-at-hand but too often overlooked. The priest is a herald and voice in the wilderness of our seemingly banal, everyday lives. The priest proclaims the present and future coming of the Lord. In the midst of life's joys and sorrows, hurts and healings, desert and lush land, the priest helps the *community* to see the God who became flesh and *continues* to so come to us. Again, Father Fischer:

> The priest interprets the silent coming of God. He interprets it not as an individual, but as a leader of the faith community. Where others see the sociological or political or psychological or family or personal forces and conflicts at work, he must see with the eyes of faith the presence and activity of God . . . in whatever he does, the priest is confirming for the community and the world the presence of God in all things. (*Priests*)

To speak about the priesthood in terms of mystery may at first blush seem to be another blow for the "diminishing priesthood." Nothing could be further from the truth. At the core of the "Catholic thing" is the sacramental view of reality (to quote Father Karl Rahner, S.J.: "Grace is everywhere") which holds that the God out there is to be found here and everywhere. St. Thomas and the scholastics would have no problem understanding God and the world in such a way. Analogy is the way we humans speak about the unspeakable and try to express the inexpressible. God works through "secondary causes," that is, through his creation. Most especially, God works through human beings. But God also comes to us through nature; the smile of a child; the hand of a friend; the loss of a loved one; and the healing we experience through reconciliation. The Sacraments are those special encounters with God in Christ which employ water, oil, bread, wine, light, darkness, fire, incense, and countless other ordinary things which carry the extraordinary grace of God. Hence, we (along with the biblical writers and the saints as well) find ourselves saying, "God is like . . . ," over and over. We don't really believe, for example, that the lighted candle at the Easter Vigil *is* Jesus Christ. Rather, we are able to make a real association (what Father David Tracy calls "the analogical imagination") between Jesus Christ and the light we are called to daily bring to the world. We can do this because "the earth is full of the goodness of the Lord."

The analogical imagination, when speaking of mystery, must often turn to the arts for expressive help. The rich heritage of the Catholic experience in terms of art, music, and spirituality comes from the analogical imagination in search of mystery. We Catholics know that there is more going on than meets the natural eye. More is being said and sung in the universe than these poor ears (except for Mother's ears, which hear everything — especially when Mother's ears are Irish!) can pick up. God is constantly at work with the mystery of his love, fashioning and refashioning the new heart and the new creation. Gerard Manley Hopkins (a Jesuit priest and poet — the connection of priest and poet has for too long gone unappreciated in today's seminary training and priestly ministry),

in the following lines, draws us into the mystery of God in the
sacramental mystery of creation:

> The world is charged with the grandeur of God.
> It will flame out, like shining from shook foil;
> It gathers to a greatness, like the ooze of oil
> Crushed. Why do men then now not reck his rod?
> Generations have trod, have trod, have trod;
> And all is seared with trade, bleared, smeared with toil;
> And wears man's smudge and shares man's smell: the soil
> Is bare now, nor can foot feel, being shod.
> And for all this, nature is never spent:
> There lives the dearest freshness deep down things:
> And though the last lights off the black West went
> Oh, morning, and the brown brink eastward, springs —
> Because the Holy Ghost over the bent
> World broods with warm breast and with ah! bright wings.
> ("*God's Grandeur*")

The analogical imagination, mystery, sacramental encounters, and the poetry of Gerard Manley Hopkins show no
sign of a diminished priesthood. In fact, just the opposite, for
the priest is the one raised up and called to be a man of God's
mystery for the community of faith. The priest is summoned to
uncover "the dearest freshness deep down things" which are
all around but unnoticed. The very foundations of our being are
shaken with the call to speak and celebrate the word of the
Lord. The priest as a man of mystery stands within a long
tradition. The following story is a case in point.

The Mystery of John

Zechariah and Elizabeth were faithful to each other and to
the Lord. In fact, Zechariah served the community as a priest.
The couple's reputation in the town was blameless. However,
there was one major problem — Elizabeth could not have
children. No doubt some suspected that the Lord was punish-

ing her for one of her sins or the sin of an ancestor long ago. Some advocated a theology which held that the just arm of the Lord is not short. Sooner or later, "God's going to get you." Yet, as our story unfolds, we will come to see that God's loving arm is an extension of his just arm and when God's going to get you, he wants more than just a pound of flesh. God wants our whole heart. You see, not only is this God jealous, but he is very mysterious. Just how mysterious, we are about to see.

Zechariah was the priest appointed to enter the temple and offer prayers and incense before the Lord. It seemed like just another day at the temple. But ordinary days have ways of becoming most extraordinary.

Zechariah: "I am sure the Lord likes incense, but it sure plays havoc with my sinuses."

He continued to incense the altar and then . . .

Zechariah: "Who are you? Where did you come from? It's my turn to incense the altar. Shouldn't you be outside with the others, praying?"

Gabriel: "Calm down, Zechariah. The Lord has sent me to you. I am an angel."

Zechariah: "Does the Lord want to stop the incensing because it bothers his sinuses, too?"

Gabriel (with an angelic smirk): "Not quite. The Lord has sent me to give you and Elizabeth some wonderful news."

Zechariah: "We are going to stop using incense. But I don't know why that would concern Elizabeth. Although she does get upset when I bring the odor in the house."

Gabriel: "Will you stop with all the talk about incense! I have something much more important to tell you. Your wife, Elizabeth, is going to have a child. A boy, in fact. His name will be John."

The look on Zechariah's face was something to behold. Sure, Zechariah and Elizabeth had prayed that they might have a child, but could this be true? Many questions and emotions filled Zechariah's mind and heart: confusion, joy, concern, hope, and disbelief. Although, if it was good enough for Abraham and Sarah, why not Zechariah and Elizabeth? But Zechariah had to make sure all this was on the level.

Zechariah: "Are you sure you have the right Zechariah?"

Gabriel (by now getting somewhat annoyed): "Yes, I am sure. In fact, I am standing in the presence of the Lord. For some reason, known only to him, you and Elizabeth will have a child."

Zechariah: "No doubt he will be just like me: strong, handsome, intelligent, and probably not like too much incense either."

Gabriel: "More important than all that, John will be a source of joy to you. This child is very special and will be called upon to play a very crucial role in the nation's history. In fact, he will be crucial for the world."

Zechariah: "Will he be a great man some day?"

Gabriel: "All are great who serve the Lord. He will follow the example of Elijah and the great prophets. He will call the people to conversion and preparation for the greatest of events."

Zechariah: "Just think, all of this by my boy. But, I must admit, I find it a little hard to believe. I want to believe, but you know . . . Could you give me a little sign to show me you are really from the Lord?"

Gabriel: "Sure. From now until John's birth, you will be unable to speak."

Zechariah managed to inform Elizabeth of all that had happened. Of course, she knew the angel was telling the truth in a way Zechariah never could. Elizabeth remained in her home and was visited by her relative, Mary, who was also with child. At the appointed time, Elizabeth gave birth and the child was circumcised. The name given to him was John. This caused quite a controversy, since no other relative was so named. Yet somehow, all knew that this child was special. To be in his presence was to experience a kind of awe or mystery. John and all the events leading to his birth were much talked about. One had a deep sense of God's spirit at work in this child. The question of the hour was this: "What then will this child be?" John grew in both human and spiritual maturity. He spent much of his formative years in the wilderness and came under the influence of a mysterious group called the Essenes. These years were not wasted. They would be a continual source of strength in the years ahead.

Much later, we see a large crowd gathered to see and hear a new preacher. He operates around the Jordan and calls the people to reform their lives. In addition to preaching, he also performs a water baptism. Some come to see him out of curiosity. Others come because they think he might be the Messiah. And still others come because they sense in him a mysterious presence which they attribute to God. The preacher's name is John. The following takes place one day at the banks of the Jordan River.

Daniel: "I can't believe the people come to see this guy. He is an obvious fake or madman. I guess desperate people will grasp at any straw. Don't they know we are the teachers of the Law?"

Benjamin: "I am not sure what is going on. Maybe the people are not finding in our teaching what they need in their lives. Maybe John's success highlights our failure."

Daniel: "Nonsense! This John has no formal training. He has fallen in with that radical group in the desert. The sun and sand have done strange things to those people."

Seth: "Everything about this John is strange. He just doesn't fit into our patterns. Look, the whole story of his birth is strange. You remember Zechariah and Elizabeth. Nice people, but I find it hard to believe that, at their age, they were able to have a child."

Daniel: "Maybe this John's behavior is so bizarre because his parents were so old."

Benjamin: "In spite of your sarcasm, Dan, the fact remains that the people do respond to his message. In fact, at times I have even felt . . . Well, you know . . ."

While our three men of the Law are discussing John, the crowd continues to grow. Finally, he appears. John is dressed in a garment of camel's hair with a leather girdle around his waist. He carries a big stick and a booming message to match. Today in the crowd are many Pharisees and Sadducees.

John: "Repent, for the Kingdom of heaven is at hand. You can no longer live in the same old ways. The times demand new ways of valuing and relating to one another. If you don't reform your lives today, you will miss out on what your ancestors longed to see."

Joab: "All this sounds so abstract. Why don't you tell us what you want us to do?"

John: "It's not what I want you to do. God is the one who has an ultimate claim on your hearts. You know what God wants of you. Be generous with those in need. Share your goods with those who are lacking the basics. Open your hearts and homes to those who are on the outside. Make room at your table for those who have no bread. If you have authority and power, do not abuse others. Seek righteousness and be compassionate."

Samuel (a leading Pharisee): "Do you think we need to repent and be baptized by you as well?"

John: "You brood of vipers! I am not sure there is enough water in the Jordan to wash away your sins. You'll need more than a washing by me. Someone greater than I will need to send the Spirit into your hearts for you to be renewed. It's not impossible, but it's certainly beyond my powers."

Samuel: "How dare you speak to us in such terms! Don't you know that we are the children of Abraham and the ones called to keep the people faithful to the covenant?"

John: "These stones could do a better job. I only say what I see and what the Lord commands. It's not too late for even you to be saved. But hurry. There is no later and more convenient hour."

Many came to John for baptism. One day, during his preaching and teaching, Herod Antipas, son of Herod the Great, a minor league politician, had John arrested. John is brought into the presence of Herod.

Herod: "So this is the great and mysterious John I have heard so much about. You are dressed the way they said. Is it true you eat grasshoppers, locusts, and wild honey?"

John: "You look a little fat around the middle and a little puffy around the eyes. Are you going to change your diet?"

Herod: "Excellent. They said you were feisty. I think you and I can reach an understanding."

John: "Praise the Lord! Are you going to come with me to the Jordan for a preliminary washing and then let me take you to the One who can help you be reborn?"

Herod: "Don't test my patience, John. I know you've been saying some terrible things about me and my poor wife. You should get a job with some of those tabloid magazines. Why do you do such things?"

John: "Do you think you are excused from God's law because of your position? Just the opposite. More is expected of you and Herodias. You should set an example. I don't basically like you. I love you. I must speak God's truth to your earthly power. This is the only hope you have for being saved. Give her up so both of you can be saved."

Herod:	"Your words trouble me. I wish I had not brought you here. How can I get you back to the Jordan?"
John:	"That won't solve your problem, Herod. Soon enough, I'll be crossing the Jordan and going home."
Herod:	"You're talking about returning to the desert and those strange people?"
John:	"Not quite, Herod, not quite."

Herod remained troubled by this strange and mysterious man. Herod wanted to free John so he could be released as well. But Herod lacked the moral courage to do so. At the birthday party for Herodias, her daughter, Salome, provided the entertainment. Herod was so impressed that he promised to give Salome whatever she wanted. Prompted by "mommy dearest," she requested the head of John. Herod, being a man of his word and not wanting to give a bad example for his guests, ordered the head of John brought to her. None of this should surprise us. The response of the world to God's truth is often ridicule. The response of the powerful to the mystery of God's power is hostility and death. To be called to carry and proclaim God's mystery is dangerous and unsettling. Yet those who do so faithfully are also called to live on the other side of the Jordan.

A Reflection

Unfortunately, we have come to desire our priests more in the likeness of Descartes than in the manner of Hopkins. We are more at home with priests who are comfortable with "clear and distinct ideas" than with men of mystery who tell us of the grandeur of God. While John's message was uncompromising, his method was poetic, imaginative, and analogical. John drew on the poetry of Isaiah ("the voice of one crying in the wilderness . . . the crooked shall be made straight, and the rough ways shall be made smooth"); the moral passion of the prophets

("You brood of vipers! Who warned you to flee from the wrath to come?"); and the humble spirit which allows one to see the invisible God made visible ("I baptize you with water; but he who is mightier than I is coming, the thong of whose sandals I am not worthy to untie"). John is not a man of mystery because of his strange birth, his unconventional lifestyle and diet, or even his association with the radicals in the desert. John is strange because he proclaims a strange God before us. And there is no God stranger than Yahweh-Jesus. If one is not comfortable with mystery, then the Christian story is not for you. For those not at home with mystery, the Christian story "is a tale told by an idiot filled with sound and fury but signifying nothing." However, for those who love a good mystery story, then the Christian life reveals "the dearest freshness deep down things."

The witness of Scripture, the ministry of Jesus, and the lives of those who are not gloomy saints attest to the fact that we are stuck with a strange, mysterious God. By human standards, our God is mad. Our God doesn't behave like any of the other gods. Yahweh is passionately in love with us. He runs through the desert seeking after his people. He makes covenants with this fickle lot over and over again. Yahweh pays us the highest compliment of becoming one like us. If we still fail to get the message (and often we do), Jesus tells stories about what God is like: he is a daddy whose love is so great and strong that he can wait for us to come to our senses. When we do, he bursts from the porch and celebrates our homecoming. Our God's love is so great that he leaves the ninety-nine and searches for the one who is lost. Again, our God must celebrate. The temptation is to be embarrassed by a God who does not seem to be in control of his feelings. We want to take such a God aside and say, "How could you leave the ninety-nine? They might have run away!" We find ourselves too often pouting at the attention given to prodigal brothers and sisters. However, we had best be careful that we don't persist in such things, for the words of Jesus addressed to Simon-Peter will come to us: "Get behind me, Satan! You are a hindrance to me;

for you are not on the side of God, but of men" (Mt 16:23).

Admittedly it is easier to be a priest who proclaims a God that remains in the clouds of unknowing. Such a God is free from involvement with the mess of history and the confusion of the human condition. The God who does his thing at a distance can always be excused from any responsibility. God is too busy with things divine to care about things below. The story of a watch-maker God can evoke respect, awe, and fear. But such a God can never move us to love, pray, forgive, risk rebirth, and hope. In time, we learn to do without the God who is too beyond and not enough in our midst. Priestly ministry becomes a monument to irrelevancy. Life in the Church becomes the lifeless "noise of solemn assemblies."

The God of mystery and comedy demands much more than good liturgy, a propositional faith, and an upright morality that is often uptight. The God of mystery wants to share his unbounded love with us. The God of comedy (and comedy can be very serious, if not somber, business indeed) wants us to be about proclaiming crib and cross as the true revelation of the Really Real. The God who lives in unapproachable light, the Ancient One who rides on the clouds, the Mighty One who speaks from the burning bush comes to us with all the power of a child. The God who pours himself out into our human condition is found on a cross. Between two thieves, forsaken by friends, surrounded by foes; this Man of Sorrows will also pray for forgiveness for his enemies and hand over his spirit to the Father. He will be laid in a borrowed grave. Yet there is a "fifteenth station" (Karl Rahner, S.J.), namely, the resurrection. Father Andrew Greeley and his sister, Doctor Mary Greeley Durkin, have written:

> In the Catholic narrative, then, the happy ending may occur not even on the last page of the book but on the page *after* the last page of the book, not with two out in the last of the ninth, but after the third strike has sent the Mighty Casey to the showers. The comic celebration, the reconciliations, the renewals of hope, the second chances, the

endings that hint at new beginnings: all these experiences in the human condition are — according to the Catholic story — hints of an explanation, sacraments of God, images of what God is like and subplots that reveal the key themes of the Big Story. (*How to Save the Catholic Church*)

To the mighty and the self-important, John the Baptizer was to be dismissed as an irrelevant irritant. To the religiously respectable folk, John was an embarrassment with his strange lifestyle and offensive message. John was a man of mystery who spoke about the mystery of the unbounded love of God for us. John was sent to prepare hearts for good news when the human heart is more comfortable with information or banal facts. John didn't fit the mold and he broke out of the taken-for-granted images of his day. The result was predictable — opposition and violence.

The priest today is a voice in the wilderness proclaiming mystery, comedy, hope, and grace in the midst of sin and death. In a culture which reduces reality to the visible and is under the reign of technique, the priest is out of step with his vision of the Child in a crib and a Man on a cross and an empty tomb. In an age which markets "gloom and doom," the priest offers hope, reconciliation, and newness of life. The problem with the mystery of the Catholic story is that we often find good news unbelievable. We have grown accustomed to the Doomsday Clock as it approaches our nuclear winter. While not playing fast and loose with our destructive capabilities, the priest proclaims the mystery of an "invincible summer." As the forces of death encamp around us, the priest and the Psalmist are one: "Even though I walk through the valley of the shadow of death, I fear no evil, for thou art with me; thy rod and thy staff, they comfort me." And the priest and the angel are one in questioning the world and Church: "Why do you seek the living among the dead?"

A Philosophical Note: Priesthood in Plato's Cave

Process philosopher Alfred North Whitehead once said that all of Western philosophy is but a footnote to Plato. No doubt many scholars would take exception to Whitehead's evaluation of Plato's place in Western philosophy. However, no one doubts that Plato has made a lasting contribution to our understanding of reality. One of the enduring works of Western philosophy comes from the pen of Plato, namely, *The Republic*. In this classic, Plato invites us to enter the Cave. We will hop onboard an H.G. Wells time machine and push the fast-forward button so as to enter our own Cave. We will remain faithful to Plato's allegory within our own contemporary world view.

The movie marquee offered the following message: CON-FUSED ABOUT TODAY? UNCERTAIN ABOUT TOMOR-ROW? GIVE US A CHANCE. WE'LL GIVE YOU A FU-TURE. STARTS 2:00 P.M. ADMISSION FREE.

Dave, Bob, and Jim could not help but take note of the strange message. They were used to seeing the name of the latest movie or advertisement from one of the local merchants. But this sign was unexpected. Yet it certainly spoke to their uncertainty and confusion. Each was in school and working part-time. None had a firm fix about their future. Often, they felt like an airplane hovering over the airport waiting for the perfect time to land. The commitment to land is always a bit unnerving. Since they had no firm plans that afternoon, they decided to go inside. After all, you couldn't beat the price of admission.

The theater was not too crowded, so they were able to sit in the front (obviously they were not traditional Catholics who were all sitting with Bob Eucker — "in the back row"). After a few minutes, a man appeared on the stage. He was dressed in a way that the audience had not expected. The man was clothed in a black suit with a matching black shirt and a little white tab visible around the neck. The man was a priest. The priest waited for the initial shock and buzz of the crowd to subside.

Priest: "Welcome. My name is Father Andrew Malone. Most people call me Father Andy. Some people call me by other names, but that's usually after one of my sermons."

David was a little uneasy at all this. Being Irish, he decided to speak up, as his mother had often done and told him to do as well.

David: "Excuse me, Father. Why are we here?"

Father Andy: "You're David Sullivan, I believe. That's a good question, Dave. So let me ask you, why are you here?"

David: "I read the sign outside about being uncertain and confused. That sure describes me. I wouldn't mind having a future. And like any good Irishman, I couldn't turn down a bargain. So here I am. Now, what are you selling?"

Father Andy: "How do you know I am selling anything?"

James: "I never met an Irishman who wasn't."

Father Andy: "Spoken like a true Italian, James Bono."

James: "Yes, an Italian who has been around too many Irishmen."

Father Andy (not able to control his laughter — another Irish trait): "I am not really selling anything. I am here to challenge you to think and feel about your lives and future. Some people want to make a living. Others want to make a contribution with their lives."

Bob: "In other words, we are here to get a pitch about vocations."

At this, several people in the theater started to get up and head for the exits.

Father Andy: "You must be a Scotsman."

Bob: "Robert Macgregor, if you please."

Father Andy: "Well, Robert Gregory Macgregor, please hold
that Scots tongue of yours and let me get a word
in."

Father Andy was beginning to see how difficult all this was
going to be. He took a deep breath and continued:
                  "I'd like you to come and see what the priest-
hood is about. Naturally, you would have to let
go of certain aspects of your life. You'll have to
change schools. It would require your leaving
home and making new friends."

David: "What about Maureen? Does she have to go,
too?"

Father Andy: "If you're going to give all this a chance. But try
not to see what I am calling you to in terms of
what you'll be giving up. Try to see it in terms of
a hidden treasure I am asking you to uncover.
You're not giving up Maureen or any of your
friends. They will still be your friends, but in a
new way."

Bob: "All of this sounds very risky to me. What's in it
for me? For us?"

Father Andy: "Everything. But, remember, there is nothing
you will give up that you won't receive back a
hundredfold. Now that's got to sound pretty good
to a Scotsman like you."

It was Bob's turn to smile, for he could feel the friendly needle
of Father Andy.

Father Andy: "Why don't you let me get on with the
presentation?"

James: "Are you going to make us an offer we can't
refuse?"

Father Andy: "I am going to make you an offer you are always
free to refuse. God is our Father, but not our
Godfather. You are always free to be a disciple

no longer. You are free to leave because you don't like good news, a challenge, or the adventure of the Kingdom of God. Jesus will never force you to follow him where he stays."

Bob: "All right, we'll listen to your story about priesthood. But I must tell you up front — I don't know what a priest is."

David: "I am confused, too. What is a priest?"

James: "Count me in, too. I see a lot of priests. My mother being Italian, and all that. But I must confess that I am unsure what it means to be a priest."

Father Andy: "Thank you for being honest. Unfortunately, a lot of priests are as uncertain and confused as you about what they do and who they are."

Bob: "Well, can't you give us some idea about priesthood?"

Father Andy: "I thought you would never ask. Why don't we watch this on the big screen. Hit the lights and let it roll!"

The theatre grew dark. A large screen descended from the roof. The clicking sound of a projector could be heard in the rear. A beam of light from the projector offered various images and stories about priests. The first series of images might be termed the "Going My Way" priesthood. The priest's major problem is an old, benevolent pastor. The priest's approach to problems is a song or a one-liner. There is nothing a priestly smile wouldn't overcome. Like the American hero, the "Going My Way" priest moves on to the next assignment when his work is done. He has no roots. He simply appears, does his work, and then disappears as magically as he arrives.

A second series of images appear which attempt to increase the masculine dimensions of the priesthood. The priest is a man's man. Yet beneath the no-nonsense exterior, the priest is really a soft touch. We might term these images the "Boys' Town" priesthood. This priest must contend with civic forces that have lost their conscience (and heart). Not a song, but a fist and quick temper help carry the day. The troublesome pastor is replaced by the realistic judge or newspaper editor who wishes the idealistic priest would go away.

A final series of images are shown to the audience. These are more contemporary. The priest becomes associated with the temptations of the flesh. The best known is Father Ralph of *Thorn Birds* fame (or infamy). The "Thorn Birds" priest is handsome and tormented by self-doubts and insecurities. He is never sure he was meant to be a priest. An understanding woman is often introduced to provide the point of conflict; and too often, tragedy. The "Thorn Birds" priest must often lose what is most precious before he comes to see the things that really matter.

After viewing all of these various images and stories, the lights are brought up. The screen returns to the ceiling. Father Andy appears back on stage.

Father Andy: "Why don't you stand up and stretch a bit?"

Dave: "Aren't you afraid we are all going to run away?"

Father Andy: "I've told you, you are free to leave at any time. But where would you run? To whom would you go?"

Jim: "Are we going to discuss any of this? I think I am more confused than before."

Bob: "Is this what being a priest is all about? I can't sing. My left hook is worse than my voice. But I wouldn't mind having a date with Rachel Ward."

Father Andy: "You and a million other guys. But look, I want to know what you thought and felt about these images."

Robert: "I must admit I found something appealing about the Boys' Town priest. I like people who stand for something so as not to fall for everything. We need more people, and priests are people — I think — who defend those in need."

Jim:	"We Italians are more lovers than fighters. Father Ralph does appeal to me. Although there aren't too many Rachel Wards."
Robert:	"To be honest, you don't look much like Richard Chamberlain."
David:	"The Going My Way priest is for me. There is something romantic about riding into a difficult situation and making things right. Just when people are ready to tie you down, you move on to the next challenge. That's adventure."
Jim:	"That strikes me as unrealistic. You don't really offer people anything. You give them a song, a dance, and a smile. But what happens after you move on? Also, you don't have any roots."
David:	"Well, my approach is just as realistic as your Father Ralph. Do you really expect to find Rachel Ward? Should you?"
Robert:	"You are both wimps! One of you is an entertainer and the other is looking for entertainment. Reality is helping people and fighting for a just cause."
Father Andy:	"Why is this important, Robert?"
Robert:	"Why?! Because we owe a debt for our life. We need to help others. It's our duty."
Father Andy:	"Why?"
Robert:	"Because I feel a need to do so, that's why."
Father Andy:	"What happens when you don't feel like doing it any more? Do you just go and do something you feel like doing?"
David:	"I guess there's something missing in Robert's approach."
Father Andy:	"And yours, too. Naturally, this includes you, too, Jim."
Jim:	"What's missing? I must admit that, as we discuss the images, they seem to be less real. They seem to lack a foundation. I guess the images we've seen just don't seem to endure beyond the initial experience."

David: "I think I know what you mean. Each one of
                these images seems to lack flesh and blood
                believability. I don't think my image could *keep*
                me being a priest."

Robert: "I am afraid my image could help me to start out
                being a priest. Yet it wouldn't last over the long
                haul. Father Andy asked the question I couldn't
                answer with my image. Something or someone is
                missing."

Jim: "Does this mean we aren't meant to be priests?"

Father Andy: "You give up too quickly. I thought for sure a
                world class lover like you, Jim, would keep on
                keeping on. What happened to the tough guy
                approach, Bob? Dave, you need to be more of a
                trooper. There is still one more thing I want you
                to see."

Jim: "Do you have another set of images?"

Father Andy: "Not this time. Follow me into the lobby."

Robert: "The light is hurting my eyes. I guess I have
                become used to the dimness of the theater."

Father Andy: "Your eyes will adjust."

Father Andy, Dave, Robert, and Jim find a table in the
lobby with five chairs. They sit down and share some refresh-
ments as they continue to discuss the images on the priesthood. As they are talking, Father Andy stands up and faces a
stranger coming toward the table. The man draws near . . .

Father Andy: "I am so glad you arrived. I think the guys were
                getting a little restless."

Stranger: "Did you think I wasn't coming?"

Father Andy: "Oh, no! I was just hoping it would be during my
                time in this small theater. Men, I want you to
                meet a friend of mine. This is Jesse B. Joseph."

Jesse: "Hi, men. To tell the truth, Andy and I aren't
                friends — we're cousins!"

Father Andy: "I see you haven't lost your sense of humor. I

	never was able to come close to your quick wit. You were always greater than I."
Jesse:	"You're too modest, Andy. Few people can match your preaching and service to the Lord. You know how much I appreciate all your advance work. It can be a real wilderness out there."
Father Andy:	"Before I get a big head, Jesse, let me tell you why I wanted you to meet with us. I think these guys might be interested in doing the work of the Kingdom as priests."
Robert:	"Wait a minute! Before we sign on the dotted line. Are you a priest, Jesse? I hope I can call you Jesse."
Jesse:	"My answer to both questions is yes. I am a priest. You can call me Jesse. Now let me ask each of you a question: what do you seek out of life?"
Dave:	"I can't speak for the others, but I want to be happy."
Jesse:	"How do you go about being happy?"
Jim:	"I am happy with a big bowl of my mama's pasta."
Jesse:	"I'd like to meet your mama. But, Jim, don't confuse pleasure with happiness. It's time for you to set your sights on the higher things. There's nothing wrong with pasta. But you will get hungry again. In time, you'll even get tired of eating pasta."
Dave:	"Jesse, I am happy when I sing and dance. Others just light up. I am not sure all this talk about priesthood has any room for celebrating."
Jesse:	"That's a good point, Dave. Too many Christians look unredeemed. I am sorry to say, but some priests confuse gloom and doom with good news. Unfortunately, they are gloomy saints. Good men, but without much joy. Sometimes Father Andy is accused of being 'too heavy' in his sermons."

Father Andy: "Sometimes you have to trouble the comfortable."
Jesse: "Don't be so sensitive, Andy. But getting back
                to Dave's observation, let me say that God loves
                to celebrate and throw banquets. What's really
                interesting is the guest list. You never know who
                might show up. You never know whom you'll be
                sitting next to."
Dave: "You mean I could be a priest and keep on
                celebrating?"
Jesse: "Dave, you can't be a true priest without
                celebrating. In fact, we turn down many good
                men just because they don't know how to rejoice
                and empower others to celebrate. They are good
                people but we have to find other ways for them to
                serve."
Robert: "The more you talk, the more I find the idea of
                priesthood appealing. Will I be able to finish my
                college studies and test the waters in the real
                world?"
Jim: "That's a good question. How about one more
                bowl of mama's pasta?"
Dave: "Right now, I'm taking part in a musical. It's the
                lead role. Could I wait until the spring or fall to
                give this a try?"
Jesse: "What further delays will you find next? Empty
                yesterdays are the result of missed opportunities
                today. There comes a time when you have to let
                go of pasta, the lead role, and the real world.
                You might find a food which really nourishes, a
                lead role in a new kind of musical, and the
                Really Real at work in your real world."
Robert: "You are surprisingly silent, Father Andy. I
                never knew you Irishmen could be at a loss for
                words. What do you think?"
Father Andy: "I feel you are being invited to something crucial,
                mysterious, and not to be missed. I can't give you
                any guarantee. Life is not risk free."

Jesse: "Well, I have to move on to the next town. It was good to see you, Andy. You are truly a great man. I hope to be working with each of you men soon. There is a lot of healing to do and we certainly need more healers."

Jesse gets up and departs out into the light of the main street entrance of the theater. A period of silence grips those who are left sitting at the table. Finally, Dave speaks up.

Dave: "Father Andy, I wish you had introduced us to Jesse first. The images on the screen now really seem unreal."

Robert: "I felt a genuine honesty about what Jesse had to say. He spoke a simple truth which freed me from many of my fears. I am still afraid, but I have a greater feeling of courage."

Jim: "Anybody who likes pasta can't be all bad. Really, though, I felt an inward rush as he spoke and told us about God and ourselves. There was something almost holy and, at the same time, very human about Jesse. I hope I see him again."

Father Andy: "I am sure all of you will see Jesse again. For now, are you willing to go and see what the Lord has dreamed and hoped for your lives? Are you willing to take a risk?"

All three young men and Father Andy remained in the theater talking a while longer. Finally, Jim and Dave agreed to meet Father Andy at the vocation office in the morning. However, Bob was more hesitant. He went back into the theater to look at the images once more. The next morning, Dave and Jim presented themselves at the Chancery.

Dave (speaking to the vocation office secretary): "Good morning. My name is David Sullivan and this is James Bono. We want to see Father Andrew Malone about the seminary. He's expecting us."

Secretary: "Oh yes, we've been waiting for you. I'll tell Father you're here."

After a few minutes, the door to the Vocation Director's office opens. Out comes the Director with an extended hand and a warm smile.

Priest: "Good morning, Dave and Jim. I am Father Matthew. Welcome. Father Andy and Jesse have told me all about you."
Dave: "But where is Father Andy?"
Father Matthew: "He's been reassigned to another diocese. You know what they say: a good man is hard to find and harder to keep. Father Andy told me that both of you are good men and I know Jesse is glad he found you."

Bill, Thomas, and Joey are walking by the campus auditorium one night with no special plans. A solitary young man is standing under the lamp light on the auditorium steps. He is handing out a sheet of paper to those who pass by. Some take it and read the message. Others take it and throw it to the ground. Still others take it and go inside the auditorium. Bill, Tom, and Joey each take one of the flyers. It says:

CONFUSED ABOUT TODAY?
UNCERTAIN ABOUT TOMORROW?
GIVE US A CHANCE.
WE'LL GIVE YOU A FUTURE.
STARTS NOW
ADMISSION FREE
Fr. Andy and Friend

Across the Generations

The idea(l) of priesthood only makes sense in terms of flesh and blood priests. As our three young friends (Dave, Bob, and Jim) found out, images can be initially attractive but not sustaining for the long haul. We humans need our fellow humans for support, inspiration, and challenge. Once again, we are talking about God's grace working through our very limited human condition. The idea(l) of priesthood must be made flesh in the lives of priests who are happy, holy, competent, and committed to the person of Jesus. No vocation recruitment technique can substitute for a very human priest who has given up everything knowing all the while that everything has been given him. To such a priest, the gift of a vocation is the treasure hidden in the field and the great pearl beyond price. None of this is said in order to romanticize or sentimentalize the priesthood. There are frustrations, failures, disappointments, and loneliness. Simply put, there is the Cross. But there is also resurrection along with the hope and joy of new life.

Even the most casual observer of the priesthood and vocational scenes is acquainted with the "present crisis." When all is said and written, it comes down to this: the Catholic population is increasing at the same time the number of vocations has dramatically decreased. The simplicity of this statement is not meant to trivialize the complexity of the causes and cures needed for recovery. No one has done more research or thinking about priests in the United States (often without much gratitude) than Father Andrew M. Greeley. He and his associates at the National Opinion Research Center have supplied us with the best data available, as well as some insightful "sociological interpretations" of that data.

The Catholic laity (and especially the young, contrary to the belief of many priests) value their priests and give them high marks. Gallup Polls consistently report that the clergy receive a sixty to sixty-five percent favorable rating in terms of job performance. Any politician would kill for such approval. In an insightful little book by Dr. Mary Durkin and her brother, Father Andrew Greeley (a true Irishman always knows who should get top billing) entitled *A Church To Come Home To*, they write the following about the importance of the priest in the life of the Church:

The Catholic priest is an important person in the Church. He always has been and he still is, despite the resentment caused by his well-publicized resignation and despite the often self-pitying "identity crisis." There is something "mysterious" (in the good sense of the word), even magical (again in the good sense of the word) about priests. Priests matter. Priests matter more than anyone in the Church except the spouse. Poor priestly ministry may drive people to the fringes; the ministry of a good minister makes them long to come home; and the hope that they might encounter priestly leadership with vision, taste, sensibility and courage provides powerful motivation to come home, even when one knows the odds are against finding such priestly leadership.

A question arises: if the priest is so crucial to the life of the Church and the religious imagination of the laity, why are we experiencing a vocation crisis? In order to answer this question, we need to keep in mind that the vocation crisis is really the vocation *crises*. There are two interrelated aspects: the attitudes of the Catholic family, and secondly, the priests themselves.

There has been a significant decline in the degree of pride experienced by Catholic families over a son who is (or wants to be) a priest. About fifty percent of those surveyed by Father Greeley indicated that they would be proud to have a son as a priest. This is down from the sixty percent figure before 1974. In a 1979 study, the percentage remained at about fifty percent who voiced pride in a son who is a priest. A very important factor must be mentioned, namely, the influence of the mother (a crucial vocation directress and recruiter) on vocations to the priesthood. Father Greeley writes, "pride in a priestly vocation in the family is one thing and active recruiting of young men to the priesthood . . . by a parent . . . is something quite different." The missing ingredient in vocation recruitment within the family is "the encouragement from the mother" (see *American Catholics Since the Council*).

In addition to the mother as a "reluctant recruiter," the

parish priests have also joined the ranks of "reluctant recruit-ers." Many parish priests, in fact, refuse to recruit at all. Why is this so? The painful answer is supplied by Father Greeley:

> It is the supreme irony that Catholics come home to the Church in substantial part because they are looking for the leadership of good priests precisely at the time when the priesthood seems paralyzed by an identity crisis in which many priests feel that, with the emergence of the deaconate and the so-called "lay ministries," the role of the priest grows ever less important in the Church. This paralyzing loss of nerve in the priesthood persists . . .
>
> *(A Church To Come Home To)*

This identity crisis and loss of nerve not only affects those who are looking to return to the Church, but also those who want to serve as priests. The parish priest too often comes across as a man with little self-esteem and an absence of regard for his work as a priest, and who is deeply confused about his identity as a priest. The parish priest presents an image to the young as one who lacks conviction and commitment to his calling. Hence, there is little wonder that the young do not consider a vocation. The problem of vocations do not lie with the young or the much maligned world. The vocation problem is a priests' problem.

> The vocation problem, in other words, is a priest problem and not a young person problem. Paradoxically, it would appear that precisely at a time when the preaching and counselling abilities of priests are most important to Catholics, priests themselves have relatively little regard for the importance of their own work . . . Unfortunately, perhaps because of poor communication with lay people, they do not seem to have as much confidence in the importance of their own ministry as they had in the years before the Second Vatican Council. And because of that lack of conviction of their work, they are disinclined to

invite other young men to follow them into the priesthood.
The decline is not in the importance of priestly ministry
but rather, it would seem, in priestly perception of the
importance of their own ministry.

(*American Catholics Since the Council*)

It cannot be emphasized enough that this *perception* by
the priests of their own lack of importance is *not* shown by the
laity in general and young Catholics in particular. In fact, the
empirical evidence confirms just the opposite. The Catholic
laity hold their priests in high esteem and greatly admire their
dedication. Priests are significant others in the lives of the
Catholic laity. The tragedy is that too many priests do not know
(or refuse to believe) just how significant. Until priests regain
their confidence, self-esteem, and self-respect, the Church
will continue to face a vocation crisis. There is a pronounced
correlation between clergy morale and new recruits for the
ministry. Without being overly dramatic, we can join with
Father Greeley in holding that "the clergy are in the process of
committing collective suicide because they do not have enough
confidence in themselves and their work to actively recruit
young men to follow them into the priesthood." Without question, there is an urgent need for "shepherds to speak." However, the bishops will need to expand their pronouncements to
include, along with nuclear war and economics, a word that
will rouse and inspire those who answered the call to serve as
Jesus served. Such a word is generational, for it is addressed to
priests present as well as to those who will follow tomorrow.

Paul's Testimony to Ministry

The noted Harvard psychiatrist, Erik Erikson, is one of
the pioneers of developmental psychology. The human person
must confront a series of stages in psycho-social development.
At the first stage of life, we must develop basic trust in our
relationship to our environment and significant others. At the

last stage of life, we hope to experience a sense of integrity. That is, the person of integrity has a feeling of wholeness and completeness about his or her life. Life has not been perfect or trouble-free, but it can be pronounced good. The person of integrity is at peace and is glad to have lived *that* life and become *the* person one is. A powerful example of integrity is offered for our consideration by the Apostle Paul. His life of ministerial integrity is not only important for his own well-being, but for Timothy and Titus as well.

As we struggle with various crises concerning the priest-hood, the testimony (in deed and in word) of Paul transcends space and time. The Apostle Paul is not only speaking to his two young fellow workers; he is also speaking to all who will follow Jesus. Paul's words are for us. Hence, we would not be guilty of eavesdropping if we tune in to a very touching conver-sation between Paul, Timothy, and Titus.

A man moves slowly but deliberately down a winding back street in Lystra. Most of the town's residents are behind closed doors. Some are hurrying to get home. Still others are lingering, engaging in conversation that is cautious. One speaks in guarded fashion and with an eye on the watch for unsuspected ears. Our man arrives at his destination. He knocks. The door is opened. The man goes in and the door is quickly closed. He is greeted by his two hosts. Finally, the man sits down and the conversation begins.

Timothy: "Paul, I am so glad to see you again and so honored that you found time to come and be with us."

Titus: "That goes double for me, Paul. It's a real blessing to have you spend some time with us."

Paul: "I am always glad to see my children again. And I do consider you my children. I feel responsible for you since it was I who got you involved in preaching the Gospel. But that was long ago."

Timothy: "We love and respect you with the affection of sons toward their father. Speaking of which, we could sure use some fatherly advice."

Titus: "I must admit, Paul, the ministry has its share of frustrations and disappointments. At times, I feel so discouraged and useless. For example, those Cretans can bring me to lose what little religion I have."

Timothy: "Ephesus is no picnic. The more outlandish or esoteric the teaching, the more the people seem to eat it up."

Paul: "I can certainly identify with that, Timothy. Titus, if you want to meet a community to test your patience, just think back to our work at Corinth."

Titus: "Don't forget the crowd at Galatia. Paul, you used some strong language with them."

Paul: "Yes, because they needed strong language."

Timothy: "Is it true that you sent a private letter to Barnabas apologizing for calling them 'fools'?"

Paul: "No comment."

Titus: "I've never known you not to have a comment."

Timothy: "Or a letter."

Paul: "Is this any way to treat the man who has taught you everything?"

Timothy: "If I didn't know better, I would think I had just heard an idle boast."

Titus: "As I remember, you really came down on those poor Romans for boasting."

Paul: "I can't believe I came all this way to be verbally abused. I could have returned to Corinth for that!"

This verbal sparring was something that each enjoyed and was quite good at. Yet Timothy and Titus wanted to see Paul for more serious reasons. These two young ministers of the Gospel needed the example and encouragement of Paul.

Timothy: "Paul, what most impresses us about your ministry is the fidelity you've shown. In and out of season, convenient or inconvenient, you have continued to preach Christ crucified."

Titus: "We all know you've had your share of hardships. You've spent more time in jail than some of the guards. Yet you keep on keeping on."

Timothy: "No matter how impossible your mission seems, you continue to talk about joy and grace. How do you do it?"

Paul: "You know I am not the most modest of ministers. Just ask Peter. But what I have been able to do is the result of Christ living in me. Christ has been in my life in every circumstance. He is really my wealth and strength."

Titus: "But, Paul, we don't all have such a foundation. We certainly lack your kind of conversion."

Paul: "Nonsense! Maybe it's not as dramatic, but it is as real and as solid. To be a true minister of the Gospel requires a shaking of the foundations of our certainties and well-constructed truths. We all must go through the dark night when we cannot work. We don't see clearly. But in time, through God's grace, we begin to gain some vision."

Timothy: "But when do we see clearly? When does this get easy?"

Paul: "You will never see with perfect clarity. It never gets easy. The real danger is to think you have it all together. There is no authentic ministry that is trouble-free. How boring!"

Titus: "Don't you ever get discouraged? Don't you ever wonder if you have made a difference?"

Paul: "Of course. Life in jail is not for the weak. Do you think I enjoyed every minute with the Corinthians and the Galatians? Many a night in prison, I had pause to wonder what I was doing and where all of this was going. I preached and taught the Gospel faithfully. Yet I kept receiving reports that some were teaching a new Gospel. In Corinth, they were debating even the resurrection and acting like pagans at the Eucharist."

Titus: "How did you keep your eye on the prize?"

Paul: "The Lord sent me fellow workers like you and Timothy. How can I tell you my love for the Philippians? To be honest, I really love those Corinthians. Ministry was never dull with them around."

Timothy: "Not all ministry is debating, traveling, and being confined in jail. There is a lot of time between time. I must admit that I feel the loneliness and even boredom."

Paul: "What you are feeling, Timothy, are the pains of being human. There is a zone of loneliness which is part of our all too human condition. No friend can know this part of our lives. At times, it is even unknown to us. Even God has a difficult time gaining entrance. Also, every great work requires a certain amount of loneliness. But what you are talking about is different. The ministry requires the support of a community of faith and good friends in the Lord. Too many fine followers of Jesus try to go it alone. Unfortunately, they seldom persevere. Ministry is not an individualistic performance. We need one another. So many times, whether traveling between communities or in jail, the prayers of the community sustained me. Our God is so good and loving. He never abandons us. In a deep sense, we are never really alone."

Titus: "What about the boredom? At times, much of what I find myself doing seems so unrelated to the Gospel. Ministry can seem so routine and just plain ordinary."

Paul: "It can seem that way at times. But remember that nothing done with love is ever meaningless. The smallest things, the most ordinary of activities, and the seemingly unimportant are all used by Jesus to advance the Gospel."

Timothy: "I must confess that even the so-called 'big things' we do can fall into a rut. At times, the preaching, teaching, and counseling can be just going through the motions."

Paul: "Ministry never falls into a rut. We do, however. There needs to be times when we go to a quiet place for prayer. Often, we understand our ministry in terms of action and doing. This is important. Yet much of our feelings of weariness and despair are more spiritual than physical. We cannot provide ministry if we do not know how to *receive* ministry. Of course, this is a hard lesson for all of us to learn and practice."

Titus: "I must say to you, Paul, that there is a certain seriousness about our conversation. The tone has a certain finality about it."

Timothy: "I couldn't help but notice it as well. Paul, are you holding something back from us?"

Paul: "I can't tell you everything. There must be some mystery in our relationship! Seriously, I want you to know how much I love both of you and I remember constantly in my prayers your ministry on behalf of the Gospel. Regardless of what the future holds, do not judge your ministry by its appearances. Ministry is a call to fidelity and not success. For if you are faithful to the Gospel, you will be successful in knowing Jesus and the power of his resurrection."

Timothy: "You do seem to be talking like we'll never see each other again."

Paul: "Nothing can separate us from one another, since we are united in the love of Christ and the service of the Gospel. But we don't know what the Lord has in store for us. Whatever it is, we know it is for our good. I have been faithful to the call of the Lord. I have served not through any power of mine, but through his wondrous grace. I know that others, like you, will take my place. I look forward to that day when I shall be with my Lord and Savior. The ministry has been life for me. The joys and frustrations, the little crosses and resurrections have all told me how gracious is our God. I know that one day each of you will experience this same rush of the Spirit."

Titus: "As always, Paul, I feel renewed when we have
these moments of fellowship. You and Timothy
mean much to me."
Timothy: "The same goes for me."
Paul: "Before we all start getting too sentimental, let's
keep in mind one very important thing before we
depart: the Lord remains at our side in bright days
and dark nights of the soul. At times, we may have
doubts and be aware of our many weaknesses, but
let us never forget that the Lord has called us to do
his work for *his* people. The people need us and *we*
need them. Together, we pilgrims journey in faith.
Let me just close with some words I wrote long ago:
'Who will separate us from the love of Christ? Trial,
or distress, or persecution, or hunger, or nakedness,
or danger, or the sword? . . . Yet in all this we are
more than conquerors because of him who has loved
us. For I am certain that neither death nor life,
neither angels nor principalities, neither the present
nor the future, nor powers, neither height nor depth
nor any other creature, will be able to separate us
from the love of God that comes to us in Christ Jesus,
our Lord.' "

A final series of farewells are shared along with a holy
kiss of peace. Each man returns to his dwelling place renewed
in and by the Spirit. Each minister has shared, and according
to the economics of the Kingdom, each has received in abundance. Titus will be able to face the Cretans once more.
Timothy will find the courage and wisdom to handle crafty
teachers in Ephesus. And even Paul was heard to say a kind
word or two about the Galatians — but not too loud!

An Omega Point

A priest of uncommon priestly integrity is the noted
theologian and preacher, Father Walter J. Burghardt, S.J. In a

collection of "homilies and near homilies," Father Burghardt draws on the words of Nikos Kazantzakis, who in *his* old age, offered the following: "There are three kinds of souls, three kinds of prayers. One: I am a bow in your hands, Lord. Draw me lest I rot. Two: Do not overdraw me, Lord. I shall break. Three: Overdraw me, and who cares if I break! Choose!" (See *Tell the Next Generation* by Walter J. Burghardt, S.J.)

The words of Kazantzakis apply as well to the priesthood. The priest is a bow in the Lord's hands. The temptation is great to follow Jesus on our own terms and seek to be served rather than to serve. We want the Lord to use us, but for our own benefit. Without *some* use by the Lord, we will rot. But his use is very conditional. Another temptation is to be so aware of our human limitations that our weaknesses become our excuses. We don't want Jesus or the community to expect too much from us. We identify with that part of St. Paul which speaks of earthen vessels. However, we tend to ignore the part about the "treasure we possess." Simply put, we don't want Jesus to stretch us with the demands of love. If we are overdrawn, our limitations will be held up for others to see. Rather than being strong at the broken places with God's grace, we see such brokenness as an embarrassment.

The believable priesthood is exercised by those who have the courage to say, "Overdraw me, and who cares if I break!" To be overdrawn by the Lord is to be extended beyond our human powers by the power of Divine Love. There is pain and inconvenience and risk. But the God who stretches and overdraws us is the God who knows our weakness and supplies the grace. When our human powers, skills, and wills reach their limit, our God strengthens us with love. It is in our weakness that God's grace reaches perfection. Again, Father Burghardt: "To live really is to risk everything, to smash through the boundaries that imprison us, to die stretching and reaching . . . Only in this way, I now believe, can a human being become real — by risking all for God and for man. And it is indeed a process of *becoming* — ceaseless, endless becoming."

The believable priesthood is the mystery of allowing

God's unbounded grace and love to overdraw us so as to become more human. This is anything but a call to secular humanism. The glory of God is the human person fully alive. Jesus came so that we might have life in abundance. The priest is a human being and it is through that humanity, and through our *particular* expression of that humanity, that God continues to "put on a human face." Father Robert Paul Mohan, a philosopher at Catholic University of America, has written a thoughtful little book entitled *Eternal Answers for an Anxious Age.* One of his reflections concerns the priesthood. Father Mohan writes:

> . . . it's a tragedy that we who love our life and our mission
> as Christ's priests have failed to communicate the joy of
> serving Christ to the young men of this generation as an
> alternative human lifestyle, with its sacrifices and its joys
> . . . The essential point I would like to make here is, of
> course, that our priestly vocation is simply a vocation for
> men. A man who cannot see the beauty of God's creation
> — and that includes the beauty of human love — has no
> place in the priesthood. If the giver sees no gift he brings
> to God, what indeed is he giving? If the one who serves,
> loves only the statues and the ceremonies, he would do
> much better to become a politician or an actor.

To be a priest who is believable and human is to be a person of courage. The courage required of such a priest is the courage to choose — "Overdraw me, and who cares if I break!" With these words, we place our lives at the loving disposal of God and community. Such an act of loving trust is done in worship of the One who is Alpha and Omega and who makes all things new.

VI

JUSTICE:
Pastoral Mission to Church and World

In our previous discussions, we focused our attention on more "in-house" issues: leadership, vocations, morality, and authority. Such introspection is essential for the Pilgrim People of God on the way to the New Jerusalem. Through critical (not cynical) analysis of our life together and openness to the Spirit who makes all things new, we continually heed the words of Jesus to conversion and renewal. The unexamined life is not worth living for individuals *and* institutions. Self-examination is often painful. However, pain is a sign of life and growth. The community of faith is always ready to move to a new land and leave the fishing nets of security and routine.

At the same time, there is always a danger that introspection will degenerate into narcissism. We can easily become fixed on our individual and collective navels. Introspection gone wrong through narcissism leaves us either anxious or intolerant. We can become compulsive about reform to the point at which no institution or structure has value. The value of what is, is swallowed up by the lure of tomorrow with its promise of improvement. We are not pilgrims but anxious, compulsive travellers rushing into tomorrow simply because it is tomorrow.

Introspection gone wrong through narcissism can also engender a sense of intolerance toward those who are different.

We become aware of our distinctive aspects and of how different we are in comparison to "them." Not only are we different, but we come to see ourselves as superior. In time, we may even take up arms (military or ideological) to eliminate the unbelievers. Also, our introspection can become an excuse for not being concerned about the larger picture of society and world. We become a ghetto having time and concern only for what touches on our community. We can find ourselves like the disciples at the Ascension — standing around simply gazing up at the heavens. The words of the two men in white robes are timely and timeless: "Men of Galilee, why do you stand looking into heaven? This Jesus, who was taken up from you into heaven, will come in the same way as you saw him go into heaven" (Ac 1:11). Simply put, the work of witnessing in history has begun. Now is the time to proclaim the Kingdom to the ends of the earth. Today is the acceptable moment for making disciples of all nations. We can risk leaving the ghetto and the upper room because of Jesus in the Spirit: ". . . and lo, I am with you always, to the close of the age" (Mt 28:20).

The pastoral ministry and mission of the Church extends to the whole world. The words of the risen Lord to the disciples are clear:

> All authority in heaven and on earth has been given to me. Go therefore and make disciples of all nations, baptizing them in the name of the Father and of the Son and of the Holy Spirit, teaching them to observe all that I have commanded you; and lo, I am with you always, to the close of the age. (Mt 28:18-20)

The Church, the community of faith in history, is entrusted with proclaiming the Lordship of Jesus and the Kingdom of God which is within history and is the goal of history. The Church has a mission which involves the world. The crucial question is this: In what manner shall the Church authentically relate to the world? How does the Church continue to be the Church of Jesus Christ while remaining in the world?

In 1951, the renowned Protestant theologian, H. Richard Niebuhr, wrote an important book entitled *Christ and Culture*. Professor Niebuhr outlined what he considered to be five ideal types or models, discerned from history, for the Church's relationship to the world.

The first model or type he termed *the Church against the world*. This type advocates a clear and distinct separation between Church and world. The Church is the community of grace and truth. The world is the home of sin, chaos, and lies.

The second model is *the Church of the world*. The Church does not shun the world but embraces it as part of God's love for his creation. The Church affirms the world. It is hard, at times, to distinguish between the agenda of the Church and the world. Naturally, this is its danger as well.

Thirdly, Niebuhr offers us the model of *the Church above the world*. The Church, the community of grace and supernatural truth, builds upon the world of nature and human truth or insight. The human is basically good. It is upon this basically good foundation that the supernatural gift of grace works to elevate the natural into the realm of the divine.

Fourthly, *the Church and world are in paradox*. This model recognizes the incompleteness of our present historical moment in terms of the Kingdom. The fullness of grace, truth, justice, and freedom will only come when Christ comes again in full glory. The Kingdom of God is here but not yet totally present. There is a fundamental tension between what is and what is to be. We live in the world but always as a people of hope grounded in the Lord's promise to return again in glory. We do not reject the world, but we do not give it our ultimate allegiance. We know we are sinners and yet we have been saved by the precious blood of the Word made flesh.

And finally, *the Church transforming the world* model has gained much recent popularity. This type understands the mission of the Church to be one of social, political, and economic transformation. The Church becomes the instrument of God's reordering and renewing the face of the earth. Issues of politics and economics are an important part of the Church's agenda.

All of the above-mentioned models have their strengths and weaknesses. Each has had its moment in the historical sun and contributed to the mission and ministry of the Church. Of course, no one model is ever found in its ideal or pure form. One form may predominate with a mixture of various other models or types present. While not wanting to minimize the importance of these models, it must be kept in mind that all presuppose that there is a recognition of, and relationship to, the world. Even "the Church against the world" model needs the world if for no other reason than as a point of contrast and separation.

But on a deeper and more pressing level, regardless of the model, the Church has a mission and ministry to the world. As such, the issue of justice is of utmost importance. If all belongs to the Lord and all time is in his hands, we need to be about doing the work of the Lord in space and time until he comes again in glory. The witness of Scripture and the testimony of the Church in history holds that God is a God of righteousness, holiness, and justice. The community of faith in covenant relationship with God must be about the work of justice and holiness as well.

The Second Vatican Council, in its *Pastoral Constitution on the Church in the Modern World*, issues a stirring vision of the dignity of the human person and the solidarity of the human family. This dignity and solidarity are not granted by any government but come as gracious gifts from God in whose image we are all made. The solidarity of the human family extends beyond the bounds of sex, race, creed, national origin, or political and class allegiances. The intended unity of humankind is derived from our common origin — the un-bounded, creative love of God. The document states:

> Every day human interdependence grows more tightly drawn and spreads by degrees over the whole world. As a result the common good, that is, the sum of those condi-

tions of social life which allow social groups and their individual members relatively thorough and ready access to their own fulfillment, today takes on an increasingly universal complexion and consequently involves rights and duties with respect to the whole human race. Every social group must take account of the needs and legitimate aspirations of other groups, and even of the general welfare of the entire human family . . . This social order requires constant improvement. It must be founded on truth, built on justice, and animated by love; in freedom it should grow every day toward a more human balance . . . For excessive economic and social difference between the members of the one human family, or population groups cause scandal, and militate against social justice, equity, the dignity of the human person, as well as social and international peace. (*Gaudium et Spes*)

This concern for, and recognition of, the dignity of the human person and the solidarity of the human family are essential aspects of the Gospel and Church life. In 1971, the World Synod of Bishops issued an important document entitled *Justice in the World*. Of special significance was the following: "Action on behalf of justice and participation in the transformation of the world fully appears to us as a constitutive dimension of the preaching of the Gospel or, in other words, of the Church's mission for the redemption of the human race and its liberation from every oppressive situation." Commenting on the importance of this passage, the noted priest-sociologist, Father John A. Coleman, S.J., writes:

The World Synod of Bishops charted a major new direction in the self-understanding of the mission of the Church in its 1971 document, *Justice in the World*, . . . This statement flows from several new insights in theology. Among these are the conviction that human history and the definitive reign of God ("the kingdom") converge at critical points such that the kingdom is both a goal *within* and the end *of* history. Moreover, renewed

attention to the social consequences of sin — sin's con-
gealment in structures of injustice and oppression —
alerted the bishops to the reality of a "social sin" which is
not removed by mere personal conversion of heart . . .
Liberation from structures of injustice is increasingly
seen as both the pre-condition of evangelization and its
effective consequences. For the Church's mission to liberation from structural sin is paramount to the credibility
of the Gospel's proclamation of a new creation in Christ.
Moreover, the feeling of freedom in human society, while
not removing the possibility of sin, is a prerequisite to
that freedom which alone can embrace the redemption
offered in Christ. (*An American Strategic Theology*)

The demands for justice grounded in our covenant relationship with God force us to look honestly at both American
society and the Church in America. The American bishops
took a hard look at the moral dimensions of the American
economy and economic institutional arrangements. The
bishops remind us that economics cannot be limited to policy
issues of dollars and cents or cost-benefit analysis. Economic
decisions and arrangements affect human beings. Hence,
economics raises fundamental issues of justice as related to the
dignity of the human person, the responsibility of political
leaders to foster economic justice, and the need for the Church
to offer moral guidance. The opening lines of the pastoral letter
clearly indicate that economic issues cannot be left solely to
the economist:

We are believers called to follow our Lord Jesus Christ
and proclaim his Gospel in the midst of a complex and
powerful economy. This reality poses both opportunities
and responsibilities for Catholics in the United States.
Our faith calls us to measure this economy not only by
what it produces, but also by how it touches human life
and whether it protects or undermines the dignity of the
human person. Economic decisions have human consequences and moral content; they help or hurt people,

strengthen or weaken family life, advance or diminish the
quality of justice in our land. (*Economic Justice for All:
Catholic Social Teaching and the U. S. Economy*)

The Catholic bishops, through their pastoral letter, are
rejecting a fundamental axiom of modern economic thought,
namely, that economics is an objective, value-free mechanism
which promotes efficiency and productivity. Questions of values and ethics have no place in the public discussion of
economics. The bishops reject this out of hand as an affront to
their responsibility to teach and guide in areas of faith and
morals as well as to the belief that no aspect of society is above
the sovereignty of God. The bishops are calling for a radical, a
fundamental examination of our economic relationships in
light of the Lordship of Jesus and the justice-will of God.
Sociologist Robert N. Bellah has framed the issue well:

> I believe that the economic pastoral raises important
> practical matters for discussion. But it is useless to start
> that discussion without facing the more fundamental is-
> sue: that the economic realm is not autonomous, that it
> exists under the sovereignty of God along with all the rest
> of our lives, and that economic decisions must be made,
> therefore, in the light of ethical criteria. Indeed what
> those who dismiss the letter challenge us to do may turn
> out to be a great blessing. For we cannot engage in the
> discussion in some narrow forum labeled "economic."
> We have first to vindicate our right to speak about
> economics by holding up our fundamental beliefs about
> God and the world. The bishops view their letter as a call
> for conversion (paragraph 328). We will respond best to
> the letter if we combine spiritual renewal with practical
> citizenship. By strengthening our sense of who we are as
> Christians we will increase our capacity for profound
> vision and forceful action in the economic realm.
>
> ("Resurrecting the Common Good,"
> *Commonweal*, 18 December 1987)

Before we turn our attention "to our most fundamental

beliefs about God and the world" mentioned by Professor Bellah, a brief word must be said about justice (economic and otherwise) *within* the Church. It is quite possible for us to preach and proclaim to the world and in the end find that we have not removed the plank from our own eye. The call to justice is not simply for the world or American society. The community bears a special responsibility to "hunger and thirst after justice." The World Synod of Bishops which met in 1971 (previously quoted) was keenly aware of the responsibility to be as just as we call others to be. The task of critical self-examination, at times painful, but always necessary, must be carried on by the Church. The Church must be a living example of justice and a defender of human rights *within* its communities. The document, *Justice in the World*, made this abundantly clear:

> While the Church is bound to give witness to justice she recognizes that anyone who ventures to speak to people about justice must first be just in their own eyes. Hence we must undertake an examination of the modes of acting and of the possessions and lifestyle found within the Church itself.
>
> Within the Church, rights must be preserved. No one should be deprived of ordinary rights because of association with the Church in one way or another. Those who serve their Church by their labor, including priests and religious, should receive a sufficient livelihood and enjoy that social security that is customary in their region. Lay people should be given fair wages and a system for promotion. We reiterate our recommendations that lay people should exercise more important functions with regard to Church property and should share in its administration.

The need for justice within the Church does not begin and end with issues of an economic nature. The Synod called for a greater respect of, and appreciation for, the contributions of women. Various disputes which arise in the Church must be settled by principles of fairness and by broad-based participation by laity and clergy. The Church must be a daily witness to a Gospel lifestyle of simplicity and poverty of means and manner. With great insight and courage, the retired Bishop of Fort Wayne — South Bend, William E. McManus, D.D., has written the following:

> Courage calls for the Church to be a model of what it teaches about the moral dimensions of business and economics. This courage will require going to extremes to show people that the Church is living up to its own ideals. Courage will demand a realignment of priorities, with more attention to those lower ones without which there can be no high ones. Courage may necessitate the closing or curtailment of programs that are unquestionably beyond the finances of the Church as a whole. Heaven help the Church, however, if it becomes so narrowly parochial that individual parishes, hard pressed for money, are forced to close schools, while affluent neighbors buy new bells for a Gothic bell tower.
>
> ("Getting Our House in Order: Economic Justice within the Church," from *Shepherds Speak*)

With these introductory remarks completed, it is now necessary for us to turn our attention to what Professor Bellah calls "our most fundamental beliefs about God and the world." To be specific, we will now examine the biblical concept of justice as it unfolds through the Hebrew Scriptures; Jesus and the theme of the Kingdom; and the responsibility of the Christian as a citizen of the earthly city in the Pastoral Letters.

Justice in the Hebrew Scriptures

The following discussion of justice owes a large debt to Stephen Charles Mott and his truly illuminating book, *Biblical Ethics and Social Change*. The story of God and the picture painted by the biblical writers is one of God *doing* justice. And this justice-doing by God is one of liberation. The poor and the oppressed are special to God and he responds to free them from those structures and institutions which enslave, dehumanize, and oppress. God is not indifferent to the crisis of the weak, the widow, and the orphan. When those in the community will not respond to the needs of the "wretched of the earth," Yahweh will come to their aid. Black liberation theologian, James H. Cone, goes so far as to understand the whole of Scripture as one grand testimony of God's liberating activity on behalf of the oppressed:

> Theology is language about God. *Christian* theology is language about God's liberating activity in the world on behalf of the freedom of the oppressed. Any talk about God that fails to make God's liberation of the oppressed its starting point is not Christian. It may be philosophical and have some relation to scripture, but it is not Christian. For the word "Christian" connects theology insepar- ably to God's will to set the captives free.
> ("What is Christian Theology?" from *Scripture Bulletin*, vol. XII, No. III, Summer, 1982)

The justice activity of God is *not* simply one of balancing the scales. The justice of Yahweh is *not* administered by a blindfolded Lord. Yahweh is the Lord of justice who exercises an affirmative action on behalf of the poor and the powerless. Yahweh acts on behalf of those who have no one to plead their cause. Among the more important passages in the Hebrew Bible, is the one concerning the jubilee year:

> And you shall hallow the fiftieth year, and proclaim liberty throughout the land to all its inhabitants; it shall be a jubilee for you, when each of you shall return to his property and each of you shall return to his family . . . In this year of jubilee each of you shall return to his prop- erty. And if you sell to your neighbor or buy from your neighbor, you shall not wrong one another . . . If your brother becomes poor, and sells part of his property, then his next of kin shall come and redeem what his brother has sold . . . And if your brother becomes poor, and cannot maintain himself with you, you shall maintain

him; as a stranger and a sojourner he shall live with you. Take no interest from him or increase, but fear your God; that your brother may live beside you . . . I am the Lord your God who brought you forth out of the land of Egypt to give you the land of Canaan, and to be your God. (Lv 25:10-55)

The people of the covenant cannot engage in acts or social relationships of injustice. The God of liberation and justice had acted on behalf of the Israelites when they were in bondage in Egypt. The people of the covenant must act in such a way that the story of liberation remains alive. How? By acting justly and working for liberation in a like manner. To oppress and exploit one's fellows is to forget what Yahweh had done, and, worse yet, to forget the very nature of God as just and holy.

Biblical scholar John Howard Yoder, in his book, *The Politics of Jesus*, reminds us that the jubilee year called the people to four fundamental commands: (1) leaving the soil fallow so the true source of all our bounty was the generous Lord; (2) the forgiveness of debts as a reminder that we are all in the debt of the liberating, saving grace of God; (3) those in bondage and slavery are set free in imitation of the God who liberated his people from their oppression in Egypt; and (4) the jubilee year calls for a restoration of belongings so as to practice the same generosity with which God has been generous to us.

This call for generosity through participation in the jubilee year is essential for an adequate understanding of justice. God's justice is experienced as generosity towards his people. There is no separation between love and justice. Love is the *active* aspect of justice. Love and justice are dynamic and interrelated realities of the covenant within history. Professor Mott puts it well:

Of the Hebrew words for justice, sedaqah has the sense of a gift, of abundance and generosity, and mipat also often communicates relief, release, and deliverance. It is highly significant that sedaqah is never used in Scripture to speak of God's punishment for sin. It deals with God's *positive actions in creating and preserving community*, particularly on behalf of marginal members thereof . . . The justice of God can appear in the context of judgment, as it does in the prophets. Justice may then represent God's victory for the innocent or the oppressed, the negative side of which is the defeat of the wicked or the oppressors, often described with terms other than those of justice. But our point is not that biblical justice is never punitive but rather that it is not restricted to that function. Justice is also vindication, deliverance, and creation of community. (*Biblical Ethics and Social Change*)

The best known and most oft quoted passages concerning biblical justice come by way of the prophets. And this is for good reason since, in the words of the biblical scholar Albert Gelin, P.S.S.,

The prophets were the conscience of Israel . . . the great prophets championed the weak, they never stopped denouncing oppression in every form: fraudulent transactions (Ho 12:8; Am 8:5), large landholdings (Mi 2:1-3; Ezk 22:29), venal judges (Am 5:7), enforced slavery (Ne 5:1-5), the violence of the proprietary class . . . and heartless officials, among whom must be included the kings themselves (Jr 22:13-17) . . . Poverty could never be considered a normal state, in the light of those lessons taught by the spiritual guides of the Chosen People . . . We see the poor man as a victim whom we must pity, a derelict whom we must save. (*The Poor of Yahweh*)

The biblical notion of justice is not abstract or intellectual, but concrete and physical. Biblical justice is keenly aware of the needs of the body as well as the oppression that results from social powerlessness. The prophets have little patience with academic exercises and word games when it comes to justice. People are in need and it is time for action. Delay is sinful. Justice informed by love and grace (the *hesed* or faithful love of God for his people and the need for the people of the covenant to love one another are at the center of doing justice) does not ask the question of merit but is concerned about need. The needs of each person are important because each person is important to God. The cries of the poor, oppressed, and powerless reach the ears of Yahweh *IF* the sounds are not first heard *and* responded to by the community. Biblical justice does not quibble about equal treatment in terms of social or legal expectations. There are situations and individuals who are in need of special care and love. The needs of the widow and orphan require greater attention than those of the rich and powerful. Professor Mott terms this biblical approach to justice "context-dependent."

> If such justice is to treat similar cases similarly, it must take a "context-dependent" form in which "identical treatment" is defined with reference to individual needs and capacities. If we are to fulfil the obligation to seek for all persons security of life and well-being, some individuals will need more care than others . . . The equal provision of basic rights requires unequal response to unequal needs. Justice must be partial in order to be impartial. Only by giving special attention to the poor and the downtrodden can one be said to be following "the principle of equal consideration of human interest."
> (*Biblical Ethics and Social Change*)

The following passages from the Hebrew Scriptures provide clear examples of the very concrete nature of biblical justice. The Psalmist presents the Lord as actively working for justice and caring for the lowly:

> Happy is he whose help is the God of Jacob . . .
> who keeps faith forever;
> who executes justice for the oppressed;
> who gives food to the hungry . . .
> The Lord sets the prisoners free;
> the Lord opens the eyes of the blind.
> The Lord lifts up those who are bowed down;
> the Lord loves the righteous.

> The Lord watches over the sojourners,
> he upholds the widow and the fatherless;
> but the way of the wicked he brings to ruin. (Ps 146:5-9)

The prophets Isaiah and Amos remind us that there can be no authentic worship if the covenant of justice is ignored. Yahweh cannot be "bought off" with animal sacrifices and liturgically appropriate ceremonies. The Lord requires of his people just social relationships along with appropriate cultic worship;

> Hear the word of the Lord . . .
> What to me is the multitude of your sacrifices? . . .
> I have had enough of burnt offerings of rams and the fat of fed
>   beasts . . .
> I cannot endure iniquity and solemn assembly. Your new
>   moons and your appointed feasts my soul hates . . .
> Wash yourselves . . . remove the evil of your doings . . .
> learn to do good; seek justice, correct oppression;
> defend the fatherless; plead for the widow. (Is 1:10-17)

> Thus says the Lord:
> For three transgressions of Israel, and for four I will not revoke
> the punishment;
> because they sell the righteous for silver, and the needy for a
> pair of shoes —
> they trample the head of the poor into the dust of the earth, and
> turn aside the way of the afflicted . . .
> Seek good, and not evil, that you may live . . .
> Hate evil, and love good,
> and establish justice in the gate . . .
> Take away from me the noise of your songs;
> to the melody of your harps I will not listen.
> But let justice roll down like waters;
> and righteousness like an ever-flowing stream.
>   (Am 2:6-7; 5:14-15; 23-24)

The God of justice requires a people of justice. The doing of justice is not simply the work of God. God provides the example and the grace to seek after justice, but it is left to the individual and the community to "let justice roll down like mighty waters and righteousness like an ever-flowing stream." Not only is this seeking after justice a requirement of the faith community, but *of the nation as a whole.* There is no aspect of life that escapes the reign of God and his doing of justice. The command to be about justice cannot be isolated or confined to Church or a private affair of the heart. Justice is social and historical. If the nation does not establish justice at the gate, then moral decay will follow.

The prophet Jeremiah continually warns against the arrogance of power by the mighty (kings) who believe themselves to be above the demands of justice. When there is moral "rot at the top," the decay filters down to the people as a whole. The moral illness of injustice takes hold and the nation begins to falter. The cure is nothing short of a genuine moral conversion throughout the society. Consider these words of Jeremiah:

> O house of David! Thus says the Lord: Execute justice in the morning, and deliver from the hand of the oppressor him who has been robbed, lest my wrath go forth like fire, and burn with none to quench it, because of your evil doings. (Jr 21:12)

> Hear the word of the Lord, O King of Judah, who sits on the throne of David, you, and your servants, and your people who enter these gates. Thus says the Lord: Do justice and righteousness, and deliver from the hand of the oppressor him who has been robbed. And do no wrong or violence to the alien, the fatherless, and the widow, nor shed innocent blood in this place. (Jr 22:2-3)

However, when the leadership of the king and the elders is lacking, the people decline in just relationships as well. Again, Jeremiah:

> For wicked men are found among my people;
> they lurk like fowlers lying in wait.
> They set a trap; they catch men.
> Like a basket full of birds,

their houses are full of treachery;
therefore they have become great and rich,
they have grown fat and sleek.
They know no bounds in deeds of wickedness;
they judge not with justice
the cause of the fatherless, to make it prosper,
and they do not defend the rights of the needy.
Shall I punish them for these things?
says the Lord,
and shall I not avenge myself
on a nation such as this? (Jr 5:26-29)

To conclude this section of our discussion, the following
is of the utmost importance: the God we worship and the God
who provides us with all that we need is a God whose justice is
expressed in generous love. The God of justice has established
a covenant of justice with his people. The God of justice
requires a people who are as just as he is just. This justice is
not abstract but a very concrete, compassionate concern *and
action* on behalf of all who are in need. The justice-doing of
Yahweh requires of us a sensitivity and moral courage such
that we are in solidarity with the poor, the weak, the powerless,
and all whom society considers to be of no account. We cannot
remain silent and do nothing in the face of oppression. We lift
our voices and join our resources (time, talent, and money)
with the exploited farm workers and the victims of prejudice at
home and abroad; we will not be quiet in the face of discrimina-
tion and sexism; the unborn and the elderly are our concern;
and we voice our protest against all sinful social structures
which dehumanize and exploit the human person. Any affront
to the dignity of the human person is an affront to God in whose
image we are all made. Each time a person is violated, we are
injured as well. In doing all this, and more, we give witness
that we are God's people.

Is not this the fast I choose; to loose the bonds of wickedness, to undo the things of the yoke, to let the oppressed
go free, and to break every yoke? Is it not to share your

bread with the hungry, and bring the homeless poor into your house; when you see the naked, to cover him and not to hide yourself from your own flesh? . . . If you take away from the midst of you the yoke, the pointing of the finger, and speaking wickedness, if you pour yourself out for the hungry and satisfy the desire of the afflicted, then shall your light rise in the darkness and your gloom be as the noonday. (Is 58:6-8, 9-10)

Jesus and the Kingdom

As we turn our attention to Jesus and the New Testament, we must keep in mind that the biblical story of justice is continued and perfected in the person of Jesus. The person of Jesus, and his proclamation of the Kingdom, are normative for the Christian and the community of faith. To proclaim the Kingdom of God and to profess Jesus as Lord does not remove us from the demands of social justice. In fact, we can go so far as to say that Jesus is a social ethic. The story of Jesus which we tell and retell forms the peaceable Kingdom in which we learn to live life as a gift and in mutual trust. We have no need to control, manipulate, or do violence to one another in the name of some personal or group goal. Our social relationships and structures are such that the dignity of each person is respected. The final and ultimate cost of discipleship is the willingness to love one another; most especially when the 'other' happens to be enemy, oppressor, and one who is different from me. We give up the need to control. We let the love of God come into our hearts so as to drive out all fear. Not only are our hearts changed, but all the face of the earth is renewed. In discussing the community dimensions of discipleship, Stanley Hauerwas writes:

To be a disciple is to be part of a new community, a new polity, which is formed on Jesus' obedience to the cross. The constitutions of this new polity are the Gospels . . . manuals for the training necessary to be part of the new community . . . the creation of a "world" through a story, by loving a God who has lived through Jesus' life . . . to serve as he served. Such service is not an end in itself, but reflects the Kingdom . . . This means that Christians insist on service which may appear ineffective to the world. For the service that Christians are called upon to provide does not have as its aim to make the world better, but to demonstrate that Jesus has made possible a new world, a new social order.

It is a new world because no longer does the threat of death force us into desperate measures to insure our safety or significance. A people freed from the threat of death must form a polity, because they can afford to face the truth of their existence without fear and defensiveness. They can even take the risk of having the story of a crucified Lord as their central reality. He is a strange Lord, appears powerless, but his powerlessness turns out to be the power of truth against the violence of falsehood.

                              (*A Community of Character*)

The strangeness of this Lord is clearly revealed over the issue of power. The absurdity and foolishness of Jesus is his authority without the usual assortment of powers: political, military, religious, or economic. The contest between the power of truth and the violence of falsehood is made visible in the confrontation between Jesus and Pilate. It is to that confrontation that we now turn.

Jesus has been arrested in the garden of Gethsemane. A group of Roman soldiers along with some officers of the Jewish temple police, with the help of Judas, take Jesus into custody and bring him to Annas. After a period of questioning, Jesus is brought to the praetorium. Pilate, the governor, comes out to meet Jesus and those who were to hand him over.

Pilate: "What is this man accused of doing?"
Officials: "This man goes about doing evil against God, the nation, and he challenges the authority of Rome."

Pilate: "I don't want to be bothered with this petty stuff. You have your own laws and traditions. Bring this Jesus into your own courts."

Officials: "You know we can't. We believe this man deserves death. However, our laws do not allow us to do such a thing. We must turn him over to you."

Pilate: "How moral of you! You can't put a man to death because of your laws. However, you have no second thoughts about letting me do the deed."

Officials: "We have our customs and laws. They must be respected. We have brought Jesus to you in hopes that you would obey your rules."

Pilate: "Don't lecture me about my rules and my responsibilities. I'll speak with your Jesus. The rest of you, get out!"

Pilate and Jesus enter the governor's house. Pilate has regained his composure. Pilate stares at Jesus with some amusement. The stories about Jesus have not gone unnoticed by Pilate. Jesus stands before Pilate in silence. Finally, Pilate speaks.

Pilate: "With friends like those men, you don't need enemies. Tell me, Jesus, why are you here? The leaders of your people tell me you are passing yourself off as a king. Are you the King of the Jews?"

Jesus: "Are you asking me, or making a statement? Do you recognize me as a king? Perhaps you just listen to what others say."

Pilate: "Let's get one thing straight — I didn't have you brought here. The religious leaders and respectable folk did you in. Just to look at you, I don't see you as a threat to me or to them. What have you done to bring this about?"

Jesus: "From the beginning, I preached the Kingdom of God. What is so dangerous and unsettling is the need for all people to change and have their hearts turned to the Lord. What is so frightening is the need to let go of the old securities and powers so that the Father can do his work in us. The kingship which I am and I proclaim does not belong to the world of earthly powers or principalities. The powers of the world belong to all who love darkness."

Pilate: "If your own people don't understand you, I certainly can't expect to do better. All this you have said seems to me to mean one thing — you are a king."

Jesus: "There are kings and there are kings. Your king is judged by the standards of force, armies, and the ability to make people do his will."

Pilate: "But what's wrong with that?"

Jesus: "What seems to be strength is really weakness. Earthly kings are dependent on those they control for adoration, fear, and praise. Your kings can only rule as long as they have someone or a group to oppress. Don't you see that the real power actually lies with those who are supposed to be under you? Your king must be in control. Yet this is an illusion. The real control is exercised by those whose obedience your king must have. Isn't this really weakness?"

Pilate: "And what makes you any different? What makes your kingship any more powerful? I have heard you have followers but followers are not soldiers. History is written by winners and those who control events."

Jesus: "The only lasting authority is that of the truth which frees us to understand our lives as gifts and all of creation as belonging to the Lord. The Kingdom of God is only a threat to those who fear the truth. Fear is that which keeps us oppressed. If you are honest, Pilate, you know that those who sit on mighty thrones have the greatest fear of truth. You need to open your heart and listen to the truth."

Pilate: "The only truth is what Caesar says is true. He has
more soldiers than either of us. Or both of us together. Truth is not to be found in nice words or
noble sentiments. Truth comes with swords and
soldiers and resources to pay followers. That is
truth. That is reality. What is truth? A word thrown
about by the powerless for consolation. Jesus, you
need to be a realist."

Jesus: "You ask me to think about truth in the face of
reality. Let me ask you, just what is reality? Is it
Caesar in Rome? Is it your power in Jerusalem or
that of the religious authorities? Reality tells us that
all this too shall pass. Every earthly reality stands
within the eye of time. All of this will pass. Only my
word of truth endures."

More than Pilate's sleep was disturbed. These words of
Jesus could not be dismissed easily. Pilate pronounces Jesus
innocent. Yet the crowd will have none of it. Pilate tries to
satisfy the crowd by having Jesus scourged, crowned with
thorns, and arrayed in a purple robe. The sight of Jesus only
sends the crowd into a demonic frenzy. In the name of all that is
holy, the crowd demands that the Holy One of God be put to
death. Pilate, with all of his power, finds himself afraid. He
withdraws from the crowd into the safety of his house. Once
again, it is now Pilate who is looking for a way out. The logic of
worldly power in time turns the oppressor into the oppressed
and the ruler into the one who is ruled. Pilate is on the run. He
is afraid. Strangely, Pilate finds himself asking a similar
question to that of the disciples when they first met Jesus long
ago.

Pilate: "Few passions run as hot and deep as those of
religion and superstition. I guess I miscalculated. I
was hoping that if I gave them a little flesh and
blood, that would do it. I am afraid it wasn't enough.
Jesus, let me ask you, where are you from?"

Jesus does not respond. This oppressed and afflicted man of sorrows opens not his mouth before earthly powers. In his silence, there is a testimony which transcends words. By his stripes, we are healed.

Pilate: "Why do you just stand there? Don't you have any-thing to say? You are a preacher who was able to gather crowds, move the people, and upset the com-fortable. Why will you not speak to me now?"

Jesus continues to remain silent. His witness is his pres-ence.

Pilate: "I command you to answer me. I am not playing games with you. Do you want me to turn you over to that crowd? Do you think I won't do it? I know your type. You want to be a martyr. They will soon forget you as they have come to forget all the martyrs."

In silence, Jesus looks at Pilate. Pilate is now so uncom-fortable that he jumps from his seat and begins to pace the floor. Jesus continues to be silent.

Pilate: "I have the power to have you freed or crucified. Your very life is in my hands. Don't you know this?"

Jesus lifts his head and looks intently at Pilate. He finally breaks his silence.

Jesus: "You still know so little about power. You think the source of power is with Caesar in Rome. Power comes from shouting, angry voices in the street. All of that is weakness. My life, and yours as well, is in the hands of my Father. I am before you and under your control only because my Father wills it."
Pilate: "What kind of father would allow his son to go through this?"
Jesus: "The kind of Father who rules by the power of love rather than the appeal to fear and violence. This

thirst for justice because the God of all so hungers and thirsts.
Justice and love are not political or humanistic movements,
but the work of the indwelling Spirit. Our hope is not in some
political ideology or social program, but in the Lordship of
Jesus who calls us to love one another and renew the earthly
city. Our political, social, and economic relationships are
such that they give witness to the sovereignty of God and the
Lordship of Jesus. The words of Professor Mott are once again
much to the point concerning this delicate balance between the
Kingdom of God and our life in the earthly city:

> In reaction to the liberal preoccupation with the social
> aspects of the Reign, it has become fashionable in con-
> temporary writings to state that the Reign of God is not a
> social program and that people do not bring it in. But the
> very fact that it *is* God's Reign which is already present in
> grace means that our responses cannot be passive . . . We
> receive the Reign as a gift but with it comes a demand and
> the power to meet that demand so that we can be channels
> of God's creation. The Reign of God is not a social
> program, but faithfulness to its demands for justice
> necessitates social programs and social struggle. The
> Reign, which shows up the relativity of such efforts, also
> provides the motivation and grace to carry them out.
> (*Biblical Ethics and Social Change*)

Responsible Citizenship: The Pastoral Letters

The demands for social justice do not always call for
angry protest or political revolution. The king or ruler need not
always be an oppressor. Life in the earthly city is necessary for
our humanity. Civil government through constitutional law is
charged with promoting justice, order, and the common good.
The Christian is called to play an important role in the life of
the city. Political leadership is a noble calling and those so
called are entrusted with the ideals and virtues of the community. Government need not be the enemy of the individual. In

fact, the government is to be the protector and enhancer of the good of all citizens. Government has the responsibility to create the conditions which allow for each citizen to contribute to the common good and partake of its benefits. The positive and virtuous aspects of government are central to Aquinas' view of the political community. In his important book, *Tranquillitas Ordinis*, George Weigel writes the following concerning the Thomistic view of governance:

> Thomas was thus considerably more willing than his great North African predecessor [Augustine] to look into human nature and human history for hints and traces of a Godliness that would lead human beings to live well — live gracefully — in this life. The essential, God-touched structure of the world, established by the Creator, had not been negated by original sin; and in human nature and human experience, Aquinas argued, we can find, through reason, "broad principles of a natural law which all reasonable men living human lives under the given conditions of common human existence can discern, and which is based ultimately on the eternal law in the mind of God, the creator and ruler of all."

Weigel goes on to indicate, drawing on the philosophy of Aristotle and the theology of Aquinas, that the state is natural and necessary for the individual to develop his or her humanity. The state does not merely exist in order to satisfy its own ends or to control the evil impulses of human nature under the influence of sin. The state is capable of promoting the common good and helping to foster the virtuous life; or what George F. Will calls "statecraft as soulcraft." The state does not bestow dignity on each person but recognizes and foster the importance of human life and the unique value of each human life.

The Thomistic/Aristotelian concept of the state places a great deal of moral responsibility on the political leaders of the nation. The ruler and the state, according to Aquinas, have important spiritual roles to play. That is, the ruler is to order society in such a way that each person is helped to reach his final, true end — the beatific vision of God. The great modern historian of philosophy, Frederick Copleston, teaches that Aquinas did not hold that "man has, as it were, two final ends, a temporal end which is catered for by the State and a supernatural, eternal end which is catered for by the Church: he says that man has one final end, a supernatural end, and that the business of the monarch, in his direction of earthly affairs, is to facilitate the attainment of that end." (*History of Philosophy*, vol. 2, *Medieval Philosophy: Augustine to Scotus*)

While not developing the role of the sovereign with the philosophical and theological sophistication of Aristotle and Aquinas, the Apostle Paul was keenly aware of the faith community's responsibility to live as Christians and good citizens in the earthly city. The following brief dialogue between Paul and his fellow worker for the Gospel, Timothy, adds an important dimension to the Christian's responsibility, namely, to pray for the civic leaders.

Part of our common wisdom runs like this: never discuss religion and politics if you want to have or keep friends. Our common experience teaches that religion and politics are two of the more interesting subjects in which we engage. In the following dialogue, Paul and Timothy exchange views on both religion and politics. To the best of our knowledge, they managed to remain friends.

Timothy: "Recently, a few members of my congregation were seriously troubled by the oppressiveness of the Roman authorities. Each day we hear about persecutions and arrests of our members. The temptation is great to take up the sword."

Paul: "Perhaps we should take up prayer before we rush to the streets and employ the methods of the world to fight the world."

Timothy: "Do you know how that sounds, Paul? It is hard to talk about prayer when your family and friends are being beaten and even killed!"

Paul: "Because it is hard does not mean it is useless. In

fact, I want to tell you that prayer and petitions for those in authority are essential if justice, peace, and freedom are to gain a foothold. Tell me, Timothy, how can we keep alive the memory of the Lord if we turn to violence and hatred? Are we really any better? Are we being faithful to the Cross and resurrection of Christ? I think not."

Timothy: "Prayer takes the long view. What about those who are suffering and dying at this moment? Is that fair?"

Paul: "We are a community of hope. We experience keenly the tension of God's Kingdom as here and yet to come. We take the long view because we believe that all time is in God's hands. Those who turn to violence only add to the violence in and of the world. We simply refuse to take part in such things."

Timothy: "How does prayer help us to live in a violent world?"

Paul: "We live as members of a peaceable Kingdom and a community which knows that everything belongs to God. But more to the point, we pray that those entrusted with political authority will understand their authority in terms of stewardship. That is, their authority and power are on loan. They will have to render an account of their stewardship. And so will each of us. Is our excuse for using violence that we were victims of violence? Is our rationale that the other side used violence first? Don't forget that we believe that history is the story of victims who become vindicated. Victims are restored because the One who was victim for us now lives — and this is our hope of glory."

Timothy: "Isn't God just? He can't possibly condone what is done to our communities. By doing nothing, we are actually aiding the forces of injustice and violence."

Paul: "These are important questions, though they sound more like accusations or reproaches. First of all, God is just. In fact, God is justice. However, you need to remember that God desires all to be saved.

Even those in political power are not outside of
God's salvific will. Jesus Christ died for all peoples.
It is crucial for political leaders to know the Lord
and serve him in justice and mercy. We cannot
afford the luxury or the arrogance to presume that
anyone is outside of God's saving love. Our task is to
pray and work for justice. We strive to live daily so
that all will come to acknowledge the Lordship of
Jesus and the sovereignty of God. This is not easy,
but it is necessary."

Timothy: "What you say seems so passive?"

Paul: "That's your second point which I want to address.
You assume that prayer is passive. Why? You want
immediate results and instant justice. This is simply
not the way history unfolds. Sin is real. But we do
not help overcome sin by furthering its reign of fear,
violence, and death. We lift up our voices and
implore the Spirit to renew hearts and our human
history. There is nothing passive about this. Prayer
requires courage and the willingness to hope."

Timothy: "Do you deny there are injustices?"

Paul: "Of course not. I've seen my share of jails and
hardships. But there is no perfect justice, peace,
and freedom until the Lord comes in the fullness of
his glory at the end. For now, we must accept our
responsibilities as citizens by working for the common good and praying for those entrusted with the
civic life of the community. In the face of injustice,
we must labor unceasingly to correct and renew and
reform. We must even be about the revolutionary
work of praying for justice and praying that the
hearts of the mighty will turn in humility to the Lord
of all."

The Catholic Tradition and Social Justice: A Pastoral Note

The Catholic story concerning social justice is deep and complex. Present at the beginning was the recognition of the need to care for those who lack the basic necessities of life. An important function of the deacon, and the community as a whole, was to serve the needs of the needy. Hospitality and making welcome the stranger are requirements for all who claim Jesus as Lord. St. Paul, writing to Timothy, goes so far as to teach that the widow in need is not merely to be tolerated or treated as an object of charity, but she is to be honored. "Do not rebuke an older man but exhort him as you would a father; teach younger men like brothers, older women like mothers, younger women like sisters, in all purity. Honor widows who are real widows" (1 Tm 5:1-2). The emphasis was clearly on personal witness as well as the public witness of the faith community.

As the story of the Catholic community unfolded in history, things of course became more complex. Yet what endures is the underlying spiritual motivation and grace: each of us is brother and sister to one another in Christ through the indwelling Spirit with God as our Father. The human person is made in the image and likeness of God. Each person is deserving of dignity and respect. There is no person who falls outside the horizon of our duty to love and to care. This is not a question of pure procedural justice but the call to owe no justice-debt, but the debt to love one another as Jesus loved us. Down through the ages, the Catholic tradition's concern for justice, the call to love one another, and the building of structures to advance justice have been motivated by seeing in those in need the hidden presence of Jesus. To minister to the least of our brothers and sisters is to minister to the needy Jesus.

In his excellent book, *Claims in Conflict*, Jesuit theologian David Hollenbach presents a detailed and highly readable account of the Catholic tradition of human rights. The writings of the popes, beginning with Pope John XXIII, extending to Pope John Paul II, contain the crucial theme of the Catholic tradition: the dignity of the human person. Father Hollenbach writes:

> The thread that ties all these documents together is their common concern for the protection of the dignity of the human person. In a speech delivered in May 1961, John XXIII stated that the entire modern tradition "is always dominated by one basic theme — an unshakable affirmation and vigorous defense of the dignity and rights of the human person." In John XXIII's view, human dignity is the concrete normative value which the entire tradition has attempted to defend. Respect for the dignity and worth of the person is the foundation of all the specific human rights and more general social ethical frameworks adopted by the encyclicals and other Church teachings. These rights and ethical frameworks have undergone a notable evolution and will continue to do so. But through this process all alterations have been governed by an attempt to remain responsive to human dignity and its concrete demands.

Pope John Paul II has enriched this commitment to the dignity of the human person. Such a dignity is not based on any human achievement but our fundamental relationship with Jesus Christ. It is through the Incarnation and Paschal Mystery of Jesus that each person is called to be a new creation and to help to form communities of the new creation. The Word became our poor human flesh and so elevated the dignity of the human person. Through Jesus' death and resurrection, the human person is called to an eternal life of Spirit-filled glory in the likeness of Christ. Jesuit theologian Rene Latourelle terms John Paul's encyclical, *Redemptor Hominis*, "a kind of charter of the dignity of the new man who has been brought into being by the blood of Christ." The dignity and worth of the human person is the gift of God through Jesus and the indwelling Spirit. As individual Christians and members of the faith community, we must remain responsive to the concrete needs of others: we feed the hungry, clothe the naked, make welcome the stranger, and work to build social structures which protect and enhance the dignity of all persons.

The justice and human rights tradition within the Catholic community cannot be reduced to interesting history, intellectual reflections, or the exclusive domain of popes. It must be found at the center of parish life. Religious leadership in the parish sets the tone, style, and depth of commitment for hungering and thirsting after justice. The motivation and dedication to a faith which does justice must be provided by the pastoral leadership in parish and chancery office. At the same time, the faith community provides the context for sustaining and enriching the commitment to social justice. Without pastoral leadership from priest, associate, and bishop, along with a community context for doing justice, the dangers of romanticism, sentimentality, faddism, and fanaticism can easily arise. The most powerful teaching about social justice takes place in terms of parish life itself. Father Andrew Greeley and his associates, in a perceptive book on pastoral leadership, make the following observations concerning parish life and social justice:

> The story that a parish tells about social justice in its daily life and in the ordinary dealings of the leadership with the people of the parish is a far more powerful feature of social justice than the propositions concerning social justice that the parishioners hear from the mouths of their parish priests. It is much to be feared that the greatest temptation to violate social justice that the parish clergy must resist is not the temptation to obscure the Church's social ethic lest the parishioners be offended by its demands, but the temptation to violate that social ethic in the style in which the parish is led; for the authoritarian leadership style is deeply ingrained in clerical culture and has historical roots which reach far back into the past. It is almost the "normal" style of parish leadership, the pattern into which priests fit without having to think

about it. Even if their ideology is liberal, they are still severely tempted to force their parishioners to respond to or to parrot that liberal ideology — for their own good, of course. (*Parish, Priest, and People*)

One of the most important ministries on the local parish level is preaching. Preaching for social justice requires more than words. There is a growing and gathering storm in the Church concerning the credibility of the clergy to speak about social issues. This skepticism comes from what is perceived to be a lack of intellectual competence and existential honesty. That is, the preaching for social justice requires the clergy to be knowledgeable. Pious slogans and moral righteousness will not carry the day. The Roman collar and priestly vestments do not excuse the priest from professional competency. Simply put, the clergy must know what they are talking about. Furthermore, words for justice must be given credibility by the way the priest lives and conducts parish ministry. The priest must not only preach the word, but he must give daily witness that he respects the dignity of all persons and hungers for justice and mercy.

The preaching for justice is an essential aspect of the Church's mission and the celebration of the Eucharist by the community of faith. And, at times, such a preaching and celebrating must address very specific issues and offer some concrete solutions. Needless to say, such preaching is always in danger of becoming shallow, sentimental, arrogant, and downright wrong. Humility and prudence are essential parts of homily preparation. The dean of Catholic preachers, Jesuit Father Walter J. Burghardt, S.J., in his masterful book, *Preaching: The Art and the Craft*, offers the following helpful guidelines when preaching for social justice:

1) Complex and controversial issues are not to be excluded from the pulpit simply because they are complex and controversial. The Gospel must be brought to our own time and faith community.

2) The pulpit is not the place to pontificate on complex issues. There needs to be prudence and humility in our preaching.
3) Preaching for social justice is not be confused with moralizing or self-righteous proclamations. The aim of such preaching is to educate and quicken Christian consciences.
4) I do not as a preacher take advantage of my captive audience. I may go so far as to provide other forums for which to discuss the complex issues raised in the homily. I recognize the expertise and experience of the laity.
5) We must avoid a judgmental attitude toward the congregation. We preach justice to *this* community because we love them and we need the love and faith of the community in return.
6) Finally, the just word must ring true in our lives as preachers. We are seen as just and we provide visible witness to the community of faith. In the words of Ralph Waldo Emerson: "A man's sermon should be rammed with life."

The Catholic tradition of laboring, preaching, and celebrating for a faith which does justice connects with the Incarnation. The Word became flesh as God's total, never to be taken back, commitment to the dignity of the human person. The Incarnation reminds us to pay attention to the bodily and physical demands of a justice active through love. The preached word must become flesh in the pulpit, the rectory, the home, the school, and the parish hall. Again, the words of Father Burghardt:

And so, what I put to preachers most urgently on preaching the just word goes beyond the word that is preached. I phrase it in two questions. (1) Do you *live* the just word you preach? . . . Does your just word leap forth from some experience of our sorry human condition? Is it your life that passes through the fire of your thought? (2) How do you *celebrate* the just word, the Word who *is* justice? Do the faithful sense that it is *your* body too that is being offered for them, *your* blood too that is being shed for them? From your celebration of transcendence, do they experience the God who enables them to "execute justice"? (*Preaching: The Art and the Craft*)

Firing Line: Liberation Theology

This long-awaited special edition of *Firing Line*, hosted by William F. Buckley, Jr., is about to commence. The topic is liberation theology and the guests are well-known: sociologist Peter L. Berger (*The Capitalist Revolution*), liberation theologian Gustavo Gutierrez (*Theology of Liberation*), Lutheran pastor and scholar Richard John Neuhaus (*The Catholic Moment*), Catholic layman and scholar Michael Novak (*Will It Liberate?*), and Catholic scholar George Weigel (*Tranquillitas Ordinis*). The examiner for this special program is noted educational psychologist and feminist writer Carol Gilligan (*In a Different Voice*). The familiar musical theme of *Firing Line* is now being played. After scanning the audience and the panelists, the camera focuses on Mr. Buckley. The music fades as Mr. Buckley pleases to begin.

Buckley: "Good evening and welcome to this special edition of *Firing Line*. The focus of our deliberations will be the relationship between certain Third World and liberation ways of speaking about God and the connection with Marxist-Leninist analysis. Those who advance such a theology of liberation claim that the Christian Gospel is compatible with the gospel of Marxism and its analysis of history, society, and economic arrangements. Advocates of liberation theology see no conflict between the Gospel of Jesus and the gospel of Marx. In fact, the Gospel of Jesus calls for a liberation from sinful social structures which dehumanize. Such a liberation can employ the methods of Marxist analysis. The question of violence looms large and is often left unaddressed by liberation advocates. All of these issues and more we wish to develop in the forthcoming hour."

(*Translation*: Mr. Buckley and his guests will discuss liberation theology and its relationship to the Catholic theological tradition.)

After the introduction of the guests and the examiner, Mr. Buckley proceeds with the opening question.

Buckley: "Father Gutierrez, as the founding father of liberation theology, would you briefly explain what is meant by this term?"

Gutierrez: "A number of qualifications to your request. Many had a hand in developing a theology of liberation; most notably, the poor and the powerless themselves. As theologians, we are called to reflect on the work of God in the lives of the people. And secondly, I am not sure that there is one, accepted definition of liberation theology. The pluralism of the term comes from the many forms of oppression and liberation. Having said that, I would briefly offer the following: theology of liberation starts from the bottom, that is, from the daily experience of the oppressed. The God of the Bible is the God of justice who acts on behalf of the poor and powerless. Jesus calls us to work for the justice of the Kingdom of God and for liberation. Christian theology is talk about God which involves talk about those who suffer."

Buckley: "While not wanting to minimize the need for social justice, is not liberation theology too parochial to have an impact on the universal Church?"

Gutierrez: "Liberation theology does address the situation of the oppressed and the exploited. We in Latin America happen to have more than our share of such misery. But poverty, oppression, and exploitation are worldwide. Yet it seems one of the ironies of history that the location of so much suffering will also be the location of so much healing and liberation. Our experience has much to teach the wise and learned of the world."

Buckley: "Is not that more than a little arrogant? Are you saying you have the truth and the rest of us are here to learn?"

Gutierrez: "What you detect as my arrogance is simply the reality of our situation and God's action for justice. You see, it is not my truth, but God's truth, that we must acknowledge and put into action. We need to rethink our faith in light of the demands of justice and liberation."

Buckley: "Pastor Neuhaus, you have written extensively on these complex themes. What is your reaction to Father Gutierrez?"

Neuhaus: "The experience of injustice and the sufferings of the poor cannot be denied or trivialized. Freedom is essential to human dignity. What concerns me in much of liberation theology is an absence of theology and an abundance of politics. At least, it seems to me that the political is often more prominent that the spiritual or the theological."

Gutierrez: "Faith cannot be confined to the Church or to the privacy of the heart. There is a public and political dimension to our faith. It is not only the human heart which needs to repent and be converted. Sinful social and political structures need to be reformed so as to respect the dignity of all peoples."

Neuhaus: "True enough. However, the Gospel cannot be made subordinate or dependent upon some political or ideological program. Salvation does not come through politics. The earthly powers and programs all exist *under* the judgment of the Gospel and the Kingdom."

Gutierrez: "Please remember that the Kingdom critiques and challenges *all* forms of political and social action. *All* reforms fall short of God's glory and justice. Is this true of capitalism and democracy? It seems that you and some of your colleagues reserve your criticism only for socialism and communism. Do you know that repression does exist on the right as well?"

Novak: "I would like to respond to that since I have written a great deal on the relationship between capitalism and democracy. I want to make this as clear as I can: Latin America needs a revolution. But the revolution it needs is both biblical and Catholic. The protective walls of the elites continue to keep the poor poor. You must stop looking North in anger and get on with the only revolution that will help the situation."

Gutierrez: "By revolution, you mean the use of capitalism. Are you holding your country and the so-called rich nations up to us as models of virtue to be copied?"

Novak: "Father Gutierrez, I do mean you need capitalism but capitalism connected with liberal democracy and the Catholic tradition of human rights and solidarity. Economic liberation comes by way of capitalism. Capitalism delivers the goods and draws on the creative talents of the people. Capitalism encourages independence, pluralism, and risk-taking. Above all, capitalism requires an environment of freedom. You see, capitalism is not simply an economic system. It is an idea and set of relations which require freedom and the ability to use one's talents."

Gutierrez: "You present a very idealized picture of capitalism. You make it sound like heaven on earth. No doubt it is heaven for those who own the means of production. However, for those on the bottom, the sad reality is dependency and exploitation. Your capitalism provides one with the illusion of freedom."

Novak: "What I am presenting is anything but idealized. Simply look at the economies of the world community. The nations with the highest standards of living and rising GNP's are those nations which have enacted economic institutions based on capitalist principles."

Berger: "Please allow me to add a word at this point. As a sociologist, I try my best to deal with the facts of empirical data. And what the data shows is this: industrial capitalism has generated the greatest productive power in human history. No other socio-economic system comes close to delivering the goods. The best example I can offer you is that of the so-called Four Little Dragons (South Korea, Taiwan, Hong Kong, and Singapore). Research on East Asian capitalism clearly indicates the superior productive power of industrial capitalism and its ability to raise significantly the material standard of living for large masses of people."

Novak: "Professor Berger makes an important point about the situation in East Asia. Their experience calls into question the whole dependency theory which is so often heard when discussing Latin America. The East Asian Rim experience offers powerful evidence that the movement from dependency to liberation is possible. What is required is the development of a mind-set and a political will for liberation and change. Economic liberation through capitalism will come only from the 'bottom up' and not from the 'top down.' State control must be relinquished so free enterprise can take hold. The human mind and the creative intellect are the most powerful forces for change, liberation, and economic reform."

Gutierrez: "You do not understand the situation in Latin America. We are not East Asia or North America or Europe. We are the people who suffer. Our history is one of tears and our story is one of exploitation by the principalities and powers who rule the world. You offer us a new approach. You speak of economic revolution and political change. These are merely useless abstractions. People are hungry, poor, ill cared for, abused, and filled with a sense of despair. How long do we wait with empty stomaches and outstretched hands? How long do we watch our future die with our children? How long will the Lord of history delay his judgment? How long will you ignore the voices of the poor?"

Neuhaus: "I know this will sound callous and harsh. There are no quick answers and perfect solutions in our history which is lived east of Eden. Sin is in our hearts and history. Our best efforts always fall short of perfect justice and freedom."

Gutierrez: "Don't you see how easy it is to take what you say and then conclude that, since there are no perfect solutions and we always fall short of our ideals, then we need not move beyond the present situation? This all becomes the worst kind of ideology. We provide the oppressor with a legitimation for doing nothing."

Buckley: "I know this is a crucial point of the argument. Professor Weigel, your latest book, *Tranquillitas Ordinis*, has caused a great deal of discussion and has much to say about what we can expect in terms of justice this side of the Kingdom."

Weigel: "The Catholic heritage concerning life in the political community is complex. This tradition extends from St. Augustine down to the too often neglected work of Father John Courtney Murray, S.J. This heritage or tradition is grounded in a number of key propositions which, taken together, we can term 'moderate realism.' Let me briefly mention these insights or propositions.

'One: Politics calls for rationality and moral responsibility. We human beings can build and sustain political communities which promote justice and respect the dignity of the human person. Sin is a reality, but it ought not keep us from recognizing the opportunities present for justice, freedom, and peace.

'Two: Total peace will never be completely achieved in this world. There is a tension between human possibility and human limitation. A true peace in this world must be built around the principles of personalism, the common good, and pluralism. Peace is the *tranquillitas ordinis*, that is, the dynamic social life of a community which aims toward *caritas* as a worthy end.

'Three: Finally, power should be used to achieve the common good. Power need not corrupt. This is a positive dimension, namely, the ability to creatively bring order out of chaos. Of course, all power must come under the judgment of the common good.'"

Gutierrez: "I am not disputing your reading of the tradition. I am calling for a recognition of a new experience and a new way of doing theology. We need to rethink our faith and theology in light of today's pressing concerns of poverty and human suffering. Faith cannot be an abstraction but it must touch people and bring healing."

Buckley: "The Sacred Congregation for the Faith, under Cardinal Ratzinger, issued an instruction on liberation theology. Of special concern was the wedding of Christian theology with Marxist-Leninist analysis. Such an analysis or method was rejected because of its advocacy of violence. Do you advocate violence?"

Gutierrez: "Mr. Buckley, you seem so concerned about violence in the abstract. You worry about loss of life when arguing about principles or theories. Let me ask you if you are equally concerned about the violence being done now, even as we speak? I am sure you don't think violence runs just one way. Must there not come a time when we must take up arms in order to overcome oppression? Cannot violence be so great against us that we must take arms to resist and defend higher values? Could it not be that at times we must resist by the unfortunate means of violence the advance of the truly violent? I am sure you would recognize such situations!"

Weigel: "Allow me to respond. There are instances when, as the last resort, we must take up arms in order to defend ourselves and others from unjust oppressors. However, violence is a *last* resort and is always carefully controlled or limited in terms of intensity and population. Violence must be used proportionally to the means necessary to resist. Violence must be limited only to combatants and not include the civilian population."

Gutierrez: "How does this differ from what I have suggested?"

Weigel: "The objection to employing Marxist-Leninist categories is this: violence is essential to the movement of history. The classless society comes into being through violence. All of history is the story of violence. The Christian Gospel is radically different. The movement of history is the movement of God's reconciling love made visible in Jesus and aiming toward the Kingdom of God. Not violence, but reconciliation is at the center of the Gospel. There is the radical call to make enemies friends. Even, and most especially, those who oppress must be prayed for so that they will be oppressors no more."

Gutierrez: "You make much of tradition and rightfully so. If Thomas could draw what was good out of Aristotle, and Augustine what was worthy out of Plato, why can't we draw what is good out of Marx? Perhaps much of the objection is not theological but political. The problem is one between the politics of the left and the right. My concern is to use what tools are present in order to highlight injustice and to rise above the oppression of the current order. And if Marx can help in some way, then I must do what Augustine and Aquinas have done before me."

Buckley: "I am afraid that we are running out of time. I would like to afford our examiner, Professor Gilligan of Harvard, an opportunity to respond to what has transpired."

Gilligan: "What has transpired has been intellectually interesting but humanly and morally troubling. Justice has been discussed in terms of principles, traditions, fairness, and various systems of economic distribution. What I find lacking is any sense of care, relationship, wholeness, and even love. We seem to be content with giving people their just deserts and then we can just forget them. Our justice becomes simply another way of avoiding contact and ongoing commitment. I must say that this is a very male-dominated way of structuring reality. Finally, I think we need to be aware of the oppression of women. Sexism is as oppressive and dehumanizing to women as to men. What we need is to develop a new language for speaking about justice. If you'll pardon the plug — we need to speak in a different voice, with a new vocabulary, and come to learn more from women's ways of knowing."

Buckley: "Thank you, Ms. Gilligan, and members of the panel and all of you for joining us tonight. The topic of liberation theology and the question of justice are crucial for us as a human family and a Church. While the clock indicates it is time for us to end, the real *firing line* will continue on the other side of the camera. It is in the home, Church, and cities that the work of justice and liberation theology become real. While we may disagree about means, the goal of a just, free, and peaceful world unites us in a common good work. Good night."

The above-recorded edition of *Firing Line* did not actually take place. The contents are based on various books and articles written by the panelists. The dialogue did not contain actual quotations from any author's work, but rather was a representation of the views each has expressed through various sources.

A Concluding Word: A Gospel Witness for Justice

Ours is an age which glorifies the lifestyle of the rich and famous. We honor conspicuous consumption and we often judge the worth of a thing or a person in terms of dollars and cents. Yet we must ask if we have not come to the point at which we know the price of everything but the value of nothing. Do we have the wisdom and prudence to recognize the treasure hidden in the fields of our everyday lives? Do we have the ability to see the abundant goodness of God's grace which makes everything a gift and is too often spoiled by our desire to turn gift into possession? Can we learn from the lilies of the field that human effort has its real limits and the final chapter and ultimate success of any life is written by grace? The whole of one's life goes into our response to these questions.

It is more than a bit ironic (if not tragic) that an age which worships freedom would be so enslaved to having. In a time which proclaims the need for liberation, we see so many possessed by their possessions. We equate our being with our having and possessing. Our self-worth is often defined in terms of our productivity, consumption, and the abundance of our possessions. We *are* more if we *have* more. We *are* less if we *possess* less. We are superior or inferior to others in terms of our possessions. In time, we come to worship what we own. The tragedy is that we are the ones who are owned and enslaved. To bow down before our things is to lose our freedom and dignity. We fashion for ourselves an idol that cannot give true life in abundance. We are doomed to disappointment and emptiness. Biblical scholar Luke T. Johnson offers the following insightful comments on the idolatry of possessions:

> The attractiveness of idolatry lies in its claim to manipu-late ultimate power; the folly of idolatry lies in the fact that any power which can be manipulated cannot be ultimate. The idolater says, "This which I can see and feel and handle and use, which is within my disposition, is the ultimate source of my worth, my identity, my security, my being. The power I *have* is the measurement of my value." For idolatry, Feuerbach is certainly correct — these gods are but the projection of primitive human needs. For the true God, he is absolutely wrong. Idolaters

are persons who, filled with the terror of non-being and worthlessness — the built-in threat of contingency — must construct their own worth (as the Scriptures have it), "with the works of their own hands." The truly depressing thing about idolatry is that by making the relative absolute, the contingent necessary, and the end-all that which is neither end nor all we have distorted reality — not just the "reality" outside us, but the whole orientation of ourselves in the world. Not only do we close ourselves off from the true source of our being and worth; we also close ourselves off from the very thing we worship.

(*Sharing Possessions*)

It is necessary, but not sufficient, to merely describe our illness when it comes to possessions. We must do more than critique the lifestyles of the rich and famous. We are called to give witness to a life of discipleship in Christ. Such a life of discipleship does not call us to a gloomy, world-rejecting existence. Creation is good and our being-in-the-world makes it very good and fills God with delight. The challenge is to bring our living faith to our daily living. In so doing, we use, share, and pass on what has been loaned to us. Faith helps us to see all as a gift and claim nothing as an absolute possession for self-worth or validation. Even less do we use things as weapons to control and exploit others. All is gift and all is a gift given to all to be used for the common good. We joyfully and freely follow Jesus fully realizing that in *having* no place to lay our heads, *all* is ours and more.

To make the following of Jesus our wealth is not to abandon the needs of others. Rather, we allow Jesus to be our richness in that we die to the old ways of having and possessing. We come to see and experience ourselves in a new way. We no longer need to live compulsively or frantically fearing that what we have will be taken from us. Jesus as our wealth is God's ultimate, never-to-be-taken-back gift which liberates us to risk caring and loving one another. Jesuit theologian John C. Haughey, S.J., in his important book on personal finances and Christian witness, writes:

As we have seen, the Christ who is now Paul's wealth is not simply the individual person of the Risen Christ with whom Paul longs to be one but is also the Christ who is present in the world, inextricably one with his members. In moving from living in and for themselves to living in such a way that he becomes their life and wealth, these members pass through the paschal way of being made new, undergoing what Christ experienced, and hence come to know him through the pattern of the death he suffered. (*The Holy Use of Money*)

The members of the faith community are not used or exploited to further one's career or self-worth. Fellow believers are not competitors with whom we must contest over a shrinking supply of scarce goods. By extension, the members of the community are gifts from our loving God and Father. We become rich by sharing our faith and gifts with others as others share their faith and gifts with us. There is a mutuality that brings forth a harmony of justice, peace, freedom, and love. None of this is accomplished by human effort alone and none of this is realized completely in this world. We fall short of God's glory, but through the indwelling of the Spirit, we try to live "in a way worthy of his magnificent riches in Christ Jesus" (Ph 4:18).

FURTHER READING

In addition to the various books quoted, the following will prove helpful in developing the major pastoral themes we have discussed.

Biemer, Gunter. *Newman on Tradition* (Herder and Herder, 1967).

Cabestrero, Teofilo, ed. *Faith: Conversations with Contemporary Theologians* (Orbis Books, 1977).

Clarke, Thomas E., ed. *Above Every Name. The Lordship of Christ and Social Systems* (Paulist Press, 1980).

Colson, Charles. *Kingdoms in Conflict* (William Morrow, 1987).

Curran, Charles E. *American Catholic Social Ethics* (University of Notre Dame Press, 1982).

Dulles, Avery. *The Dimensions of the Church* (Newman Press, 1967).

Greeley, Andrew M. *Uncertain Trumpet* (Sheed and Ward, 1968).

Greeley, Andrew M. and Mary Durkin. *How to Save the Catholic Church* (Viking, 1984).

Groome, Thomas H. *Christian Religious Education* (Harper & Row, 1980).

Happold, F.C. *Religious Faith & Twentieth-Century Man* (Crossroad, 1981).

Kavanaugh, John Francis. *Following Christ in a Consumer Society* (Orbis Books, 1982).

Keane, Philip S. *Christian Ethics & Imagination* (Paulist Press, 1984).

Kelsey, Morton T. *Caring* (Paulist Press, 1981).

Kennedy, Eugene C. *Comfort My People* (Sheed and Ward, 1968).

Keyes, Paul T. *Pastoral Presence and the Diocesan Priest* (Affirmation Books, 1978).

Lebacqz, Karen. *Justice in an Unjust World* (Augsburg Press, 1987).

_____. *Six Theories of Justice* (Augsburg Press, 1986).

Meehan, Francis X. *A Contemporary Social Spirituality* (Orbis Books, 1982).

Metz, Johanne Baptist. *Faith in History & Society* (Crossroad, 1980).

Miller, J. Michael. *What Are They Saying About Papal Primacy?* (Paulist Press, 1983).

Moran, Gabriel. *No Ladder to the Sky* (Harper & Row, 1987).

Rahner, Karl and Karl-Heinz Weger. *Our Christian Faith. Answers for the Future* (Crossroad, 1981).

Rahner, Karl. *The Practice of Faith* (Crossroad , 1983).

Schillebeeckx, Edward. *Ministry* (Crossroad, 1981).

Schlossberg, Herbert. *Idols for Destruction* (Thomas Nelson, 1983).

Sullivan, Francis A. *Magisterium* (Paulist Press, 1983).

Yoder, John Howard. *The Priestly Kingdom* (University of Notre Dame Press, 1984).